Praise for *Left*

Belinda Subraman does not hold back. Her poetry is fierce, tactile, lucid, and metaphysical, exploring life and death relentlessly, all the while recording both the suffering and the joy that is intrinsic to nature. Her poetry is compassionate, its nakedness our lesson and reflection. *In Left Hand Dharma,* Subraman embraces the phenomenological realm and assails inequity without shame. She lets us know when beauty is pierced by indifference or blatant cruelty. *Left Hand Dharma* unleashes upon the reader energy conjured by art and meditation. These poems are native to an inspired and tireless worker, they are the revelations of a traveller. They mark a learned path, a way we must go to find out. We have no choice but to follow.

—Michael Rothenberg, author of *Drawing The Shade* and *Wake Up and Dream*

Belinda Subraman cautions that "nothing can be said that is news," and she is correct. The mysteries of birth and life, sex and death, joy, deprivation, the sacred and the profane, have been with us always. The trick lies in coming to these things with the grace of unguarded honesty and the courage to tell what one knows. In another life, Subraman would maybe be a shaman or a sage, tucked away in a cave, reading the future through bones scattered around a communal fire. She understands so damned much. This collection is a victory, a celebration of a career well-spent chasing the word across distant lands and the chasm between human lives. It is a wellspring of blest water. Prepare yourself and drink.

—Jeff Weddle, Eudora Welty Prize winning author of *Bohemian New Orleans: The Story of the Outsider and Loujon Press*

Belinda Subraman ponders the hard questions: honesty, physical autonomy, personal choice, spiritual practice versus dogmatic religions, geo-politics. Her poems also deftly and subtly describe the impact poverty, mental illness, physical infirmities, and aging have on individual lives. Subraman's scope is broad enough to use physics to interrogate the impact of age on a woman's place in a world of predatory and unkind forces. Yet her voice is intimate enough to draw a clear and compelling image of that North Carolina country girl growing up fast as a young adult in India, Germany, and travels elsewhere, to finally find her home in the US/Mexico borderlands. Her poems are a delight to read.

—Donna Snyder, author of *The Tongue Has Its Secrets* and coordinator of the Tumblewords Project

Belinda Subraman's *Left Hand Dharma* reminds us that poetry is not only found in life's daily routines, such as the grinding repetition of work, but also in existences that turn into "watercolors" of constant discovery. This omnibus also urges us to pay attention to the "now" before we arrive "already gone" into oblivions. In the end, Subraman's first-rate work attests to poetry's power to capture and transcend the ordinary world, and that's a trip worth taking.

—Lawrence Welsh, author of *Begging for Vultures: New and Selected Poems, 1994-2009*

Belinda's life long dedication to the arts and gentle spirit infuse both her work and her arts community. She is an important voice: quiet, sensitive, compassionate—a voice needed in every time, but especially now.

—Su Zi, editor/publisher of Red Mare

In her opening poem, "Buckling the Bible Belt," Belinda Subraman pledges allegiance to her hillbilly past but goes on to quote Melville, "Silence is only the voice of God." She takes the reader through incarnations of this holy silence and its often dark and damaged place in the world. "A Drunk Holy Man teaches Humility" and:

> We celebrate life in the cemetery.
> We eat with the dying.
> We laugh with the dying.
> We are the dying.

yet her poems are vividly alive and pull us from the silence.

In "Crazy Like a Poet" the speaker tells us:

> with or without drugs
> I go on like Shakespeare
> writing dialog
> for a nest of fairies
>
> under haloed mimosa trees.

Subraman does much more than create fairy dialogue. Her poems stand as shrines to the body and spirit calling out to memory: as a woodpecker tree or as the scent of polka dots her grandmother wore, or as:

> Time is God passing through me
> [...]
> where a memory blurred into everything
> becomes a light that blinds us into one
> [...]
> beyond orgasm and beliefs.

This collection reads backwards to earlier poems where we see the promise that led to her recent work. The most poignant, inspired by her position as a nurse from the chapbook: *Late Night in the Psyche Ward*, and earlier ones from the chapbook *Notes of a Human Warehouse Engineer* about her job as a CNA in an El Paso, Texas nursing home. Her poet's eye and layered compassion for the patients allow the reader into rooms where the mirror reveals the tragedy of aging and dementia. I realize her loneliness, she writes in "Gloria wants to call the police," while one resident sings:

> My heart is so filled with love,
> I could die.

But I see Subraman's work echoing from "Mrs. Estrada is 98":

> This lady will not slip away quietly,
> lay down her ghost and leave us.
> She will be found grasping the bed rails
> trying to get up to live.

Left Hand Dharma is an evocative body of work by a uncommon poet, a compassionate observer and participant who hears the silence and answers.

—Anne Elezabeth Pluto, author of *Benign Protection* and *Lubbock Electric*

Left Hand Dharma

New and Selected Poems
by Belinda Subraman

Left Hand Dharma

New and Selected Poems
by Belinda Subraman

Unlikely Books
www.UnlikelyStories.org
New Orleans, Louisiana

Left Hand Dharma: New and Selected Poems

ISBN 978-0-9988925-7-3

Eighteen Dollars US

First Printing

Unlikely Books
www.UnlikelyStories.org
New Orleans, Louisiana

To Keith Thompson,
who knows how far I'd go for a blizzard.

The Order in Which They Appear

from *The Innocents*

from *The Jesuit Poems*

from *Skin Divers*

from *He Dreams His Playmate*

from *Eye of the Beast*

Notes of a Human Warehouse Engineer

Acknowledgements

Some of these poems have appeared in the following print and online publications: *Amelia, American Poetry Journal, Alpha Beat Soup, Amelia, Asylum, Big Bridge, Black Bear Review, Bloodstone, Borderlands, Best Texas Writing, Caprice, The Chachalaca Review, Chiron Review, Coal City Review, Conditioned Response, Dog River Review, Dusty Dog, Fennel Stalk, Gargoyle, Heaven Bone, Howling Dog, Louisiana Review, Ikon, Lummox, Muses: Words into Music, Nerve Cowboy, Mezcla: Art and Writings from the Tumbleweeds Project, Newspaper Tree, Ourobouros, Poetry Breakfast, Puerto del Sol, Nixes Mate, Open, Pearl, Poets&Artists, Pressure Press Presents, Psychopoetica, Ramingo's Porch, Raw Bone, Red Fez, Red Mare, Return to Mago, Ristau: A Journal of Being, Rio Grande Review, Sin Fronteras, Slipstream, Unlikely Stories, Vox Feminae: Woman as Creator and Created, The Writing Disorder, Yellow Chair Review,* and *Xenophilia.*

A few of the literary people who have made a direct impact on me through publication and/or correspondence and who influenced or encouraged me during the early stages of Vergin' Press and Gypsy Literary Magazine include Robert Burlingame, Lyn Lifshin, Judson Crews, Arden Tice, S. Ramnath, Ron Androla, Cheryl Townsend, Hugh Fox, Kurt Nimmo, Peter Magliocco, Andy Robson, Michael Hathaway, Mark Weber, Todd Moore and Gerald Locklin.

From early in the 21st century I've known Jonathan Penton, publisher of Unlikely Books, through politics and poetry. In fact, I first met him at an anti-war protest and a few months later he told me about his online magazine. This was before *Unlikely Stories* published books but it was clearly a goal he had in mind. I count him as a good friend as well as a literary pal and excellent editor.

In the past few years I've appreciated Jeff Weddle's literary friendship, from having me as a subject in one of his Master's classes, being interviewed for a new literary project and his general good attitude and support of the small press. We also read each other's poems and books.

Su Zi, poet, artist and publisher of *Red Mare* came into my life a few years ago through my *Gypsy Art Show* blog. She became a regular contributor of essays on building community through the arts. Turns out we both had Etsy shops and we ordered each other's art and crafts. We bought each other's books and read each other's work. Before she left for the New Orleans Poetry Festival she called me up to read a brand new long poem: strong, brave, gritty and impressive. She made me #12 in her Red Mare Series of handbound chapbooks.

Many thanks to *Poetry Breakfast* for nominating me for Best of the Net, 2017.

The cover art, "Angel/Goddess," is by me and signed prints are available from my shop:
https://www.etsy.com/shop/mysticalhouse

Introduction

In the 6th grade, in the 1960s, in a small town in the northwest corner of North Carolina, I awoke to poetry and became fascinated with the impact a skillful arrangement of words, sounds and meaning could have. I began to make my first poems. Oh, they were prosaic rhymes no doubt, about patriotism and religion, but give a ten-year-old in the Bible Belt a break.

In the 7th grade my themes expanded. I began to write little humorous bits. I remember the last four lines of one piece: "One morn as I went/ to change the sheets on his bed / I found Dear John / on his dirty sheets dead." Some of my little poems were passed around in class and a few people seemed impressed. I had never had that reaction before in my strict, punitive upbringing. But I knew early on that I was a writer because I had a burning passion to be one, not because of any false prospect of fame, money or even encouragement. It was something a very shy child could do. I felt as though the air shimmered around me when I wrote something that seemed to work well.

In high school I subscribed to *Writer's Digest*. I thought it somehow connected me to the world of writers with their own shimmering atmospheres. I remember that Judson Jerome was then the Poetry Editor. In about ten years I would be mentioned several times, quoted and reviewed in this magazine. A few years after that I would have a full page feature in *Writer's Digest's Novel and Short Story Market* as the editor of *Gypsy* magazine.

My first publication was as a freshman in college. There was a box in the library where you could submit your literary writing to the campus arts magazine. With a racing heart I dropped some of my poems in it. In a few months I was amazed to see them published in a nice format.

A few years later, I began regularly submitting to literary magazines. I quickly learned the sting of rejection, but although it depressed me, it didn't stop me from submitting. I had a few successes here and there. Like any writer I felt elevated to hold a publication containing my work.

In 1982, while living in Germany, and after having bought a dubbing machine, I got the idea to ask poets and musicians from all over to send their work on cassette. I would make a master tape, copy it, and send it back to contributors and subscribers. I called this *Sanctuary Tape Series*.

In early 1983, still in Germany, and after having corresponded with several editors of small literary magazines, I decided to start my own *Gypsy Literary Arts* magazine. Several editors gave me helpful ideas and people to contact for my first issue. Ron Androla was particularly helpful. I believe he was the one to give me Charles Bukowski's address. Seems like everyone I wrote to sent work. Bukowski told me to just toss out whatever I didn't use and I did. Somehow in my insulated little world I missed the part about him being famous. Not long after that the movie *Barfly*, written by Bukowski and starring Mickey Rourke and Faye Dunaway, came out.

I "typeset" the issues myself. I had a state-of-the-art typewriter with font wheels I could change out. I had only three choices though. I also used rub-on lettering for titles and clip art here and there. During this time it seemed everyone was doing collages, including me, so there were collages in a lot of the first issues. After

I had my layout ready I would seek a German printer. Most every issue was from a different printer and had a different style but it fit with the "gypsy" image.

Word spread fast through the small-press community. I was inundated with manuscripts from many countries. I received a photo and interview with William Burroughs early on. I received work from people who had been on the *New York Times* Bestseller List. Some issues would have representation from like ten countries. I had twenty university subscriptions and maybe seventy other subscriptions at the height of it all.

In the mid-80s I started receiving poems, and then personal letters and sexy pictures, from the Vatican. Came with the Vatican's seal and everything. He was a horny Jesuit with an abstinence vow. Turns out he was pursuing several other long-haired poets at the time. This is how I met Lyn Lifshin. I received a manuscript from her filled with the same words he'd used with me. She described him perfectly. I asked her if his name started with a T and we started quite a correspondence which lasted a few years. One night, about 0300 my time, she interviewed me transatlantically on a New York radio station.

In the early 90s I received a letter on professional business stationary with fancy letterhead from a lawyer threatening to sue me for using the word "gypsy" as the name of the magazine. It was from a Romani anti-defamation league. I couldn't take this seriously—"gypsy" has several meanings, and they admitted they had not seen the magazine.

Publication politics wore on me over the years. I quickly learned that all editors were writers too, although not necessarily good ones. Also, these were the days of snail mail only and it was always requested and expected that you send a self-addressed stamped envelope, an S.A.S.E., to return your work and editor's note on your submission. Many didn't. This meant I would have to pay to return it or I would not return it at all. We editors considered it a big insult—inclusion was the simplest courtesy on the writer's part. Once, when I returned a manuscript at my expense, I asked the writer to be sure and send an S.A.S.E. next time. Instead they sent a postage-due envelope with twenty-five pennies in it as an insult. Postage-due mail was not rare. Eventually I would refuse to accept them as the writing within was as unpolished as the sender's manners.

When I moved back to El Paso, Texas in 1989 I began connecting with writers and poets in person. My husband, Ramnath, and I spent many weekends with Judson Crews in Albuquerque. He knew a lot of well-known poets before they landed in our college textbooks and had edited several small-press magazines. He had spent a year living next to Henry Miller who received a steady stream of famous visitors. He gave me a vast stream-of-consciousness memoir of hundreds of pages and gave me permission to do whatever I wanted to with it. In 1992 I published, under the Vergin' Press imprint, a small book called *Henry Miller and My Big Sur Days*. For a while I had quite a few orders from libraries and collectors. Within a couple of years I got a letter from Bell and Howell promising to keep it in print and to send me a stated amount of the cover price for every copy sold. It sounded like a good idea but I never saw a penny. I learned years later they had sold the rights to someone else and I was completely cut out of the picture.

I published *Gypsy* as well as Vergin' Press books for ten years. My last regular issue was in 1994. At that time my marriage was ending and I went to nursing school so I could support myself. I lost interest in publishing others and concentrated on polishing and submitting my own writing. Before the inevitable big move in my life I submitted several boxes of letters, pictures, and publications to my archive at the University of New Mexico at Albuquerque where they remain. If you were a writer, and wrote to me during this time, you may very well be in that collection.

By the mid-90s I had been in over 500 print publications—everything from Xeroxed micro-publications to university and scholarly journals. I got my first computer in 2000. Within a year or so it finally dawned on me that I could search for a person by name and I would receive info on them. This is how I discovered Ron Androla again, who by then had an active writer's group called Pressure Press. It was a great group, but I didn't have much time to participate, as I was now a Registered Nurse working in hospice. It meant forty-hour work weeks plus many on-call nights. I was frequently jolted out of bed in the middle of the night, to hurriedly dress and travel up to 50 miles to pronounce death, comfort a family, do the necessary paperwork, report to the medical examiner, wait for the body to be picked up and then get back to my apartment around daybreak just to go back to the office at 0800. On-call duty had no pay except for the time I was actually with a patient, but the interrupted sleep pattern threw me off for days. I hasten to add that hospice work was the most fulfilling work I ever did. I grew vastly as a compassionate human being.

While I was preparing for nursing school and working as a nursing aide I wrote a series of poems called *Notes of a Human Warehouse Engineer*. It won a small competition with a prize of $100 and chapbook publication. Later, I chronicled my first nursing job at a psych hospital in *Late Night in the Psych Ward*, which was also published.

My print submissions fell off rapidly after I got used to the computer. I started appearing in online publications. For a long while I had a website and on one of the pages I would put live links to my online publications. But the links would go bad and publications would disappear. At least with print magazines you had something tangible. Still, both formats had advantages. I published a few issues of *Gypsy* online but it was too much for me with very little free time. I did put out one more print edition of *Gypsy* around 2003. It cost a mint and very few people saw it. I knew it would be my last.

When I finally thought to Google my own name, I found a lot of recordings of my own voice, set to music. I had read many of my poems onto tape in Germany, and Ken Clinger had put them to his own music. The recordings were now up on several music sites. So when I got out of print publishing, I got fascinated with podcasting. I knew it was just sharing sound files, but coming from the snail-mail, low-circulation days it was magical that anyone in the world could hear your voice at any time they wanted.

In my first experiences in podcasting, I was interviewed by others. Simon Toon of *Slam Idol* in England interviewed me. In an interview with Will Brown of *Cloudy Day Arts* I realized that my *Sanctuary Tape Series* had been a sort of "ancient" podcasting. After that I started interviewing others.

I found myself racing home from hospice, still on-call, to contact my subject at the agreed-upon time. I was exhilarated, talking to talented and sometimes famous people. I interviewed Pulitzer Prize winners;

authors from big publishing houses; a shoe designer who had been a friend of Andy Warhol; a 1960s pop star, Billy Joe Royal (Down in the Boondocks); an outstanding musician, Peter Buffet, whose dad used to be the richest man in the world; a four-time National Poetry Slam winner, Patricia Smith; Ravi Shankar; an American Nurse Practitioner in Afghanistan and a host of others. For a while my interviews were carried on three online radio stations, two of them in England.

I met Jonathan Penton in 2003 at an Iraq War Protest in El Paso. I had been seeing his name a lot on an online activist group we both belonged to so when I heard someone call out for a Jonathan and he answered I was pretty sure that was him. I went over to introduce myself and we became friends. He started attending Green Party meetings which I hosted. After a while I discovered he was the editor of one of the very first online literary magazines called *Unlikely Stories* which was founded last century and continues to this day. He was in contact with a multitude of poets and soon I was hosting some of them as they came through town on reading tours. I also hosted a Green Party Presidential candidate, a Green Party Gubernatorial candidate and a folksinger around this time. Did I mention I was still working in hospice, still on-call, still podcasting, writing a bit, was a busy activist and Green Party co-chair of El Paso and on the State Executive Committee?

In 2007 I quit hospice. Coincidentally I met Sylva that very same day. She was referred to me by a poet living in England, named Gerald England. She emailed me that she was a poet, happened to be living in my town and had stage IV liver cancer. We quickly arranged a meeting. She looked healthier than most people; a vivacious German beauty. She was into metaphysics and denial, as long as was possible.

Sylvia introduced me into New Age therapies, such as Reiki, and ancient wisdom written by men with long, hard-to-pronounce names. Soon after meeting we recorded our poetry together, and produced podcasts about poetry and life. She published a book, *In the Garden of Illness*, and did a book signing at Barnes and Nobles. I enlisted an artist friend to write a book review which appeared in the *El Paso Times*. She taught a writing workshop for the Tumblewords Project, a workshop series in El Paso. I made a web site for her. Ironically, she said she had to be dying to feel this alive!

My experiences with Sylvia as well as being my own father's hospice nurse are covered in more detail in my last book, *Blue Rooms, Black Holes, White Lights,* which is still available from Amazon.

While I continued nursing and writing I kept up a number of websites. *Gypsy Art Show* was a hodgepodge of reviews, insights, essays, art and opinion. I had guest columnists, two of which were regulars for a while, Bari Kennedy, a Naropa graduate who had hobnobbed with the Beats, and Su Zi, a poet, writer, publisher, artist and award-winning horse woman. *GAS* went on nearly 10 years. It would still be a thing but someone parading as Google sold me a domain name in the last year or so and when it came time to renew, there simply was no way to do so. I would follow links that would dead-end. Every avenue I tried was unsuccessful. My blog and the years of work that went into it disappeared. Of course they tried to sell it back to me for $5,000! Even if it had included the work that had been lost I could not pay that. But that was only the domain name. I let several other websites go on my own accord for different reasons. My only regular site use now is on Facebook and Instagram.

I met my current husband, Keith Thompson, at a New Year's Eve party in 2010 at his house where I now live. Another quirky, intelligent, left-handed blondie. Early on we made our own drums in a workshop and started going to drum circles. It was the sound vibrating through our bodies synchronized with the vibration of others and the swirl of energy it created in the group that hooked us. At times I could hear, from far away, otherworldly singing. I would look around to see if anyone's lips were moving. But it was some other phenomenon. I can't know for sure what makes this happen but I've searched for info and I know others have experienced it. It is awe-inspiring is all I know for sure.

It wasn't long before we found an African drum class, led by Erick Hickerson. At this writing we have been with the African drumming community for five years. A couple of times a years, our teacher's teacher, Soriba Fofana, originally from Guinea, comes to El Paso to teach us. Every Sunday for the past several years we drum on Sundays, learning new rhythms. We also drum for the African dance class that follows. From April to October we participate in a free form drum group called Echoes in the Park. We go to other towns also to participate in special drum gatherings. At times wherever I'm drumming, when everything is synchronistic, I still hear "the angels sing." Our teacher, Erick, actually does sing at times but that's a different sound.

As far back as I can remember I have always loved to create things. I think I owe this to my Grandmother Elledge who lived across the street from me while growing up. She knitted, crocheted, made all sorts of crafts and I would ask he to teach me each one.

When I was thirteen I crocheted a huge afghan and and sewed a patchwork quilt top which my daughters have now. I also learned papier-mâché, Swedish embroidery, and doll making from her.

Over the years I have done stained glass, semi-realistic painting, sculpture in cast stone and bronze, bead work, feather work, soap making and vegan skin care to name a few. The past couple of years I have been doing experimental techniques in acrylic painting and alcohol inks and have sold a few. Artists fascinate me. I understand the joy of process, the discovery of self that inevitably occurs and the certain amount of daring it takes to attempt it.

For several reasons, I'm in the process of cleaning my storage unit. I am re-discovering a lifetime of poetry. Much of it still stands and worthy of seeing light. Over the next couple of years I will slowly sift through it and type up the worthy pieces and hopefully you will get to read them later on.

Finally, I discovered yoga this year. The trendy BS and what I thought were exaggerated claims put me off for decades. I tried several studios before landing in my yoga home at the YWCA with a teacher with many years experience, Betty Jiron. In only a few months I see my body and mind slowly transforming and I am grateful to have overcome my needless prejudice against it. So, from a standing tree position I wish you health and happiness. Namaste.

Left Hand Dharma

New Poems

Buckling the Bible Belt

I pledge allegiance to my hillbilly past
cheap fan motor buzz
black dirt harshness
inbred bullies and bigotry.
Winter baseboard rumbles heat
in thin walls of fear
walls that work as refuge
enshrine weakness with
corporal punishment in tombs of shame.
Echoes down a backwards hall
require humility and magic prayer
as earth boils and fumes in science.
Reason is a devil's turd
as we eat the flesh of white Jesus
and drink his blood.
Crackers and grape juice with guilt
and submissive independence
whirlpool around inherited drains
one slang language misunderstood
bucked up with guns
and ambivalent Bibles for all.
Amen.

Humidity and Jesus

In the hot, damp South of last century
when a noisy metal fan
was our technology for cooling
when digital only meant fingering
where guilt and shame
were on a playground for Jesus
who turned water into wine
but made it a sin to drink.
Even symbolic blood, in church
was grape juice, body of Christ a cracker
to be eaten while sweating
in punishing wood pews.

Some men never came in
melted anywhere without rules
where moonshine was medicine
without angry women crocheting
quilting and canning
praying or saying they did.

There were tears in the house
assurance of God's forgiveness
for being human
mouthing code
no one dared disdain...
energetically charged interpretations
with tendrils of longing
clinging metaphorical feathers
from the ghost of a spaceship
stuck in reverse in the rain.

Clutching the Known

"Silence is the only voice of God,"
Melville said.
Hence TVs, stereos, mouths,
industrial noises
are always going
as if life were busy work
to keep us from knowing

In the end it's all nothing
nothing we're aware of

not even silence.

The voice of wind
blows over one's grave.
"Alone" goes into a further phase.

Who would hurry
to a higher ignorance?

Note to My Surgeon: Bedside Manner

I have man-made holes
stuck together with glue
I feel my insides pressing outward
I wear a brace for balance
to hold the weak muscle wall steady.
Every act of violence seen hurts me.
Every touch feels rough.

Surgeon, no one has done to you
what you did to me.
Don't tell people they don't need
what you're going to take
and how you're going to scrape
one organ off another
like you're not going to paralyze their muscles
and shove a pipe of air down their throats
keeping them close to death
as you try to save them.

You downplayed recovery so much
I wonder what's wrong with me
three weeks later.
Man, you cut me, four times.
You took away a part of me
forever

made me vulnerable
with wounds and pain
and told me three days is all I needed.

But I am not Jesus, neither are you
and he probably wasn't either.

Having Won the War on Christmas

Just another day with
heavy coercive joy
hung in cold holiday air.
Memory's an aching comfort
on the edge of despair
from the days when senses scrambled
and echoed thunder
living between altered worlds
and confusion.

Our dead fathers teach us
hoarding memories in a time vault
is a deception as we fade.
We always have with us
what we think we've lost.

Lunch With Jesus

We held hands around the table
at Applebee's and prayed before eating.
Fox Network was there and low self-esteem.
"The white cops were right," they chanted.
"More people need beating,
We need more guns.
Too many getting rich off welfare
too lazy to work."
"Christians have no rights," one claimed.
"What about the Christians?"
I kept quiet. Dogs were howling for meat.
Jesus turned his head away.
Bibles slept in their cars.

I’ll Fly Away, Oh Lord

We prayed to the wizard
with the hickory stick
greedy to live past expiration
with the bigots of Sunday
mumbling hymns before football
under the oppressive eye of god
and regulating relatives
tortured forever with love.

Drunk Holy Man Teaches Humility

Dogs were penned in
with dirt and weeds
where a lawn might have been.

At night the dogs howled
afraid or just screaming
to the animals of night.

Fear was in the house.
Speech was discouraged
to keep from setting off
the man of fire
who would lash and scorch
then burn you down.

There were threats,
always "don't tell."
Fear and shame
tainted our blood.

Our world was tight-fisted
with just enough love
to keep fear from swallowing

just enough love to learn
the heart can burst.

Dia de los Muertos

Every twist and turn,
psychotic thrill
and ghostly energy
find their way into
the movies of our lives.
Each sequel better than the last.
Each year the art better.

I function in a senior reality.
The future is obvious.
I choose to Be
awash and overwhelmed
with the maps through time,
a spiritual topography.

The part of me that felt apart
is now at one with Being, softly.
I let go of so much, willingly.

The first half of our years
energy heightens
and the last half it eases
into a fuel of memories, wisdom
and a desire to beam back
love for Life, for what is, for Being.

We celebrate life in the cemetery.
We eat with the dying.
We laugh with the dying.
We are the dying.

Dying

Fire bolt lights our senses.
We leave with thought vapor
climatic desire
mutated time explosions.
Universal air drifts in
leaving animated shells
turning stone body lava
into earth again.
Disoriented free falling sieves
of dodecahedron light
spins a portal open
in a wall of fog
and we become the sky
tripping osmotic worlds
across mythological interpretations.

Sounds of Slavery

It's the sound of an
O_2 concentrator or liquid air
being forced in
through tubes and masks
through membranes to tissues
keeping cells alive
and withering.
It's the sound of a feeding machine
slowly turning its wheels
forcing food through a g-tube
in the belly of a would-be corpse
kept grotesquely alive.
It's medical infliction
of ultimate control.
It's the sound of wailing
from fear of defeat,
of endings,
of the unknown,
just before realizing
one can postpone
tears for the dying
by plugging them in for years.

They say it's because they love them.
They even say it in court.
Yet no one alive would wish for
the sentence they impose
and denying that life is temporary
is no evidence of love.

Refugee

A little boy asleep on the shore
fell from a boat where he swam like a fish
but he was no fish.

His family, lured by dreams
of kindness somewhere,
a day without blood and splattered brain matter,
an electric chance of new and better
where children build castles in the sand
where the sound of water is calm and soothing
and children do not drown
looking for a safe place to play.

Fog Window

I accept my strangeness
big loves faded

memories spill
on a messy desk

disbelieving all
that could be my cane

anxiety kaleidoscopes
wet voltage

knowing excites
dreams in a river

the idea of India
is taffy in the bend
of a warm spiced pull

memories warp into mood
belief in all stages

time is weather

life is a watercolor
of angels in the rain

Crazy Like a Poet

We walk with
ghosts on a raw ego highway
breathe in the dust of all that lives
and the origin of stars
velvet vibrations
in theatrical clouds

holding the line between worlds
holding a yin-yang pendant
over its astral core

where events shatter myths
of who anyone is...

like me, with Venice sliding by
on the last voyage with my mother
in youthful confusion
still living with open
alien airwave sensors
breathing color, smelling design
straddling words.

With or without drugs
I go on like Shakespeare
writing dialog
for a nest of fairies

under haloed mimosa trees.

Dissection of a Thought Balloon

I sense my grandmothers.
I am now the age
they always seemed to be
with stern blood understanding
once removed from the sting of judgment.

Wisdom nods unconventionally
seasoned by tolerant love
compassionate wishes
ancestral salutes
through antique scents of creaking floors
of mulch and cannabis.

The breeze heavy with Earth's kiss
reminds me the trees were my friends
their nuts and leaves my toys.

Childhood obsessions
dreams of desire
turn inside out.

Autumn freshness
wombs inward
toward the fire.

Lesson: Meditation

Wisdom unsheathes
in artistic abandon.
That which purpose forces
splits the truth.
Scheduled Zen pins air to a wall.
Every second, a different story.
Forget date, time, place and mat.
Sit on the face of the earth
and *open*.
It will come.

Fractured Peonies

I became
black beans boiling
in a witch's kettle
on an open fire

I became
nautilus swirling inward
bird as fish in the sky

when he said he loved my body
implying but not me.

Memory Is a Woodpecker Tree

We snuggle down for the cold
joyous greed and mercy
in carols of nebulous infinite love
and slaughter
where Biblical yin-yang
produces branding codes
tethered to twelve layers of selves
half of them lovers
half of them trees
unnaturally used for torture
and cartoon sweetness.

Zen gelatinous cauliflower magic
constructs reality as a river,
illusion with no legs
where everything is wet
and not one drop matters more
than another.

Trees with holes
leak sap eaten
and recycled by birds
who nourish life underground
life that eats our death
when the coffins rot
and what we thought we were becomes
feces from thousands of worms.

Our Nature

Run from the rain with me
not the kind that mists—
cooling kisses
or even reluctant drops
but the kind that slams and stings
awakening our bodies to wetness
seeking shelter in tangling limbs
under a mothering Mulberry tree.

Monsoon

I

The heavy sky applauds our roof.
I walk out to soak
to receive the universe
a lover in the rain.

II

Water deepens and brightens,
falls softly, enthusiastically.
I open like the desert
dropping clothes on the ground.
Wet is beautiful.

III

Back porch leaks to its own beat,
irregular time on a rustic chair.
Waves and waves of darkened sky play on.

Dreaming in the Tub Room

Where my well-worn wooden Buddha
meets your two-toned Himalayan salt lamp
under the wall-size carving of a mandala
we know nothing beyond sensing
our cell puppies dancing with passion
in the contrasting weather water
in the indoor and outdoor tub room
where times bleeds and flows
under the stars through a screen to infinity
where we win the sex Olympics
in our age category
and my howling is timed
on illegal CIA porn TV

Science of Getting Up

The rooster awakens
at the first orange glow
in a deep blue mystery.

Is it the warming air
or is it the glare on chicken vision?
Is he happy and celebrating?
Bragging? Complaining?
Or do the juicy atoms stimulate
his poultry maleness.
and arouse his crow?

How can we know
the weight of sunlight
on a sleeping cock?

Progress in a Ship of Moon and Stars

Our corkscrewing choice is
superhero complex or top-heavy greed
in a dynasty of bucks-in-bed economy

living on controlled mind grids
bombarded by 4K TV rays and
cellophane wrinkles of reality

Associative synesthesia
is some of this strangeness
an empath with a radical mind
sensual transportation to parallel worlds...

The universe expands
to keep me stimulated
protected by smoke rings
on Mars.

The Innocent and the Awkward

In the heat of my Southern youth
with a body blooming but no explanations
where night life sounds blush with humidity
I collect bugs with lit up-rumps
in a large mason jar and put holes in the lid.

A pop singer appears on TV
with a voice sweating sweet sex
and a soul-sucking inward need.
Telescoping backwards
through a dream haze
I would have a crush on him
in undefined fantasy.

I would feel electric tingles
and be confused.
Repression was a coffin of lust.

I was no more sexy than
lightening bugs in a bottle
could make a good lamp.

Unseen Proof

I am settling the chaotic atmosphere
where membranes are penetrated
where electric ions and magical molecules
swim in a sea of energy
among plant-people with bitter minds
hoarders of myth, hiked up egos
clinging to rumors in an ancient book
that many misread.

Veils are lifted as the skin thins
and the body travels among
differing tongues.

Hope is in the shadow of ghosts
after youth disappears.
Innocence is the heart of the universe.
I release the burden
of passion and pain.
Every moment is in awe
of what the last one brought.
I savor reflections on events,
but not mirrors, as I near
transformation of my essence
when I will fertilize flowers
and be beautiful again
rooted in another brief forever
jiggling with atoms of joy.

To My Palestinian Hero

Jordan.

Machine gun dreams by the Dead Sea
Hyper reality near the bones of Moses.
Every mile there were guards and guns.
I had forgotten my passport in tribal lands.
A Texas license saved me
and a guard who would rather eat lunch
than clean up blood
and create paperwork with explanations.
I floated in two inches of melted salt
that became sticky crystals in my hair:
Biblical dandruff
movable seasoning
Lot's wife in defiance.

A Palestinian at the Golan Heights
near the Syrian border saved us.
He spoke Arabic to our driver.
There was animated conversation
then the Palestinian began
speaking English to us.
He said our driver planned
to abandon us
just past the Syrian border.
We had trusted him.
We bought his lunch at the Dead Sea
laughed at each other's pantomime.
Now everything changed.
He knew we knew.

We asked to go to Amman,
back to the American Study Center
where there were gates, 24 hour guards
with uniforms and automatics.
Maybe he thought we were diplomats
worth something somewhere...
a myth in a fairytale wrapped in a dream.
Just two RNs learning about refugees
planning to tell their stories to the world,
misunderstood by a refugee driver
working illegally
saved by a man whose country had been stolen
who saw the innocence of two white grannies
and revealed the plot to us.
To him, I am always grateful
even if this is my imagination.

Ojo Caliente, New Mexico

Sun cracked grass signals
the yellow haze of transition.
Pinon fire in a kiva stove
is a Southwest desert Fall
in the armpits of tradition
and passionate drumming.

Precarious rocks cling
on an overhead cliff.
Mesquite and Sage
breeze by geckos.

Steam rises
in the lithium pool:
Aura eggs meet
spiritual nutrition.
Fairy wings tickle
the unmentionable.

Spa police say
"Whisper, please.
Respect the sacred water."
We think of Standing Rock.
We are awed
in the presence
of the liquid god
and its protectors.

We are silent
as hummingbirds.

Synesthesia and "The River Song"

Age four I was called
by the wounded earth smell
of a freshly trimmed hedge
the way honey sounds
under a full moon breathing
my grandma's scent of polka dots.

At the portal to fluid reality
my karma scope cast
lights of glad kindness
and legends seeping through me.

I remember sickness
every childhood disease
and talking to aliens
(probably delirious with fever)
but I remember there was magic
in a mimosa tree
and a belting for sharing
knowledge of my anointment.

They cut the tree down
and forbade the utterance
of anything not Biblical.
I said little for years
afraid of my tongue
and shadows greater than my own.

I'm past the noise of tidiness,
posted regulations
through 40 translations
and constant derailment
of what I might have been
without cruelty and jumbled senses.

From tasting pain in everything
picked and dying to now
it is the voice of the rock
not the river I hear
with cinnamon periscope eye.

Poets Murdering Nova

Laws of physics allow magic
to move Space-time math
from a wormhole in the dust
of my Beltane shoes.

A mind-mist crinkle of a dream
spirals time, transporting
a poem to a probability wave
of electrons and art.

A prolific Space-time poet
smoking Dark Energy
creates Big Bangs
and multi-verses daily.

Where heaven is a string
of quarks creating poems,
extra dimensions of space
make invisible
vibrational patterns;
misty propeller roses
around the heart
where all one imagines lives.

Orgasm and Belief

Time is God passing through me
with hurricane mirrors
in the weight of sunshine.
Time becomes
photos in misplaced envelopes
with names we've mostly forgotten
remnants in a crumbling catalog
turning digital membrane
then glorious air jazz
searing the senses
over flowering cacti and desert daises
where the odd deer walk the wild beyond

where I can feel grateful
a sense of wisdom
moments of peace
where a memory blurred into everything
becomes a light that blinds us into one
where random chime breezes
breathe positively
beyond orgasm and beliefs

like God, you know
passing through me.

New Year's Day

My back hurts from moving furniture,
a week of scrubbing the house,
gathering supplies, making food
for a four-hour party.

The tree's still up and moaning.
Lumens flash to waken.
No way my eyes can touch
the myths of winter.
The kitty knocks Jesus
out of his swaddling clothes.
The daze is over.

She now sleeps in
the crook of my arm
one leg extended in a hug.
I am blessed by snoring fur
ready for the jaws of January.

Peace on Earth

We exist in wisdom that speaks in rain
leaves that rattle on the ground
hot stares from the sun

where dreams photograph
momentous wells of un-remembrance
in the essence soup of all things.

We are electrons in overwhelming mass
the warmth and light of embers
high birds on a roof perch

peaceful insignificance
the melding of yin and yang

Om across the cosmic sea.

Thoughts and Prayers

I want a church
but not the established kind
where members brag about their guns,
see war as a game where God takes sides,
where ancient history is props for killing
and congregations are one color.

I want one family under the sun
revolving on a rock together
in a spiraling galaxy of mystery and awe.
I want a Church of Earth, hugged in clouds
where respect belongs to positive energy
never to the armed and threatening.

I want fear to dissipate and the hate it creates.
I want weapons to fly out of all hands
with magnetic, irresistible forces of love.
So I wish with all of my Being:
May relief in the knowledge of our connection
fill the gap where your automatics have been.

Meddling Women

The father was an Army Private
who rarely came home.
The mother
was the life of a party
somewhere else.
Two children under five
were abandoned
twenty hours at a time.
The little girl would call me, crying,
saying she was afraid, hungry.
I read books to her,
told her to be brave.
This happened every day
until, burning,
I called Captain Somebody,
the father's boss.

But he wouldn't touch it.
This was the Army.
Didn't I know that?
His job was preventing war.
Kids without parents...
what did that have to do with war?

My Religion

I was raised by paradox
and Southern tunnel vision
where God was a magic word
who mostly brought beatings
when we gave a damn.
There was power in a book
of weird translations
that made no sense
that everyone swore by.
The bigger and fancier the Bible
the holier you were esteemed.
Fancy church ladies had
flowers and lace hugging
unregulated misogyny
and rules few followed
but claimed they'd die for.
Even as a child in Sunday School
I could never make sense
of the Trinity
or how God as Jesus
could "die for us"
or how dying could
take away sins we
didn't know we'd made.
Seeking clarification
itself was a sin...
was the devil whispering.

I remained “a good girl”
until college and Philosophy 101
when my entire belief system
crashed into history.
Stolen myths
with names changed.
God was a plagiarist
mean and proud
warring for possessions
under holy pretense
and a hypocrite
breaking the rules
enforced on us.
Of course He was us.
We made him in our image.

Yet I hold reverence
for the mystery of Life:
infinity that boggles the mind
our webbed connections
and roots of Love.
I call this God.
I believe.

Inheritance

We're bubbles of energy
in meat suits
collecting heaps of metal
crippling countries for oil
refusing to believe
we're killing the earth,
all for the glint of gold
fat numbers on a screen
that is ours temporarily
then passed on
along with dying land
to our children who hate us
because we did not love anything
including them, enough.

Beyond Meaning

There's a seeming realness of grounded thought
and an awkward fit of another human
in our dream.
We can share space and agree
to be tolerant of illusion.
We can agree to share some meaning in our lives.

Meaning is the weight in our heads.
It could be excessive rumination
the looped reels of life
or the invisible force behind our acting out
the dream that makes us crazy or calm
or sure of what could never be but is.
Meaning is the assignment of the soul.

We long for the fire of illusion
that does not contradict
our earthbound reality
but rides along on a higher plane
something that sparks the aura
tingles the essence and
sends vibrations through the cosmos.

We long for the embodiment of love
torn between blissful numbness
and the excitement of too much stimulation
and weighted expectations
all for reasons we do not realize
are substitutes for what we can not know.

Faith

We are dots on a globe
that sustains us.
Our understanding decreases
as historical, hysterical notes
chronicle a human infestation.

The earth cracks, erupts,
bleeds in lava,
cries hurricanes,
wails tsunamis.

We stab and drill inside her
empty her bowels of oil
replace with toxic water
as if she were not living
and we didn't poison mother.

Our cauliflower ears
coffee and sea-blue eyes
register desire
propped by dogma of dominion
exalted to gods
who enslave their own.

Look, I never gave up altars
but I never gave up reason.

If I just spread my arms,
open my hands
as if to fly like the angel
I believe I am,
my faith will not save me.

My lack will haunt me.
I will fall in the reality
of gravity
as my mind soars.

I may not believe in science
but it believes in me.

Selected Poems from

Blue Rooms, Black Holes, White Lights

Unlikely Books
First Edition: 2009
Second Edition: 2016

Blue Room

Wildlife flickers above the fan.
A hummingbird approaches.
A plane lands on the wall.
A lace wedding cake flutters in the breeze.

Buddha appears with light and stone.
Ashes surround the pagoda.
A book and father lie waiting.
The fame of love is framed
above a door's encryption.
A camel prances with a prince and a woman.
Flowers are mistaken.
A change of season brings armies and storms.

A tall thin bookcase holds
a Moroccan rug down.
An Italian bed holds up the dog and pillows.
The TV is blind without birds.
Tiny life takes over.
A thousand calls of night paint the mood.

Thin caskets of words and sound
slide into frames.
Neon sculptures dip down from the ceiling.
A hum of blades disturb the throat.
Hands tilt upwards.
Nothing can be said that is news.

A corner is filled with mosaic nakedness.
Santa sits near a fairy and a beer
above a steeple in a bookshelf of dreams.
A folding angel hovers over flowers
and a sweet but angry man.

Kleenex unfolds and catches.
The pink column of myth and wood
supports air and possibilities.
A tree lamp grows under mirrors.
A woman meditates, floating.
Her breast wears hats from many lands.
Her crotch is laid with red tile.

Moths thump the beaded sameness
of a hat-framed lamp.
A purple dragon across the room
shines with amethyst eyes.
Bugs and the dog fade as soon
as light turns inward.

A change of season brings armies and storms.
A thousand calls of night paint the mood.
Nothing can be said that is news.

Issues, Colors

I can no longer tell
the color of pale walls.
They all seem to have a touch
of green or blue
but I am told they are white or gray.
What trick of reflection is this
that I can tint walls
with my mind?

My father asks,
"It won't be long now, will it?"
My mother says, "Don't tell me.
I can't think about it."
I deny denial
and simply see color
where there is none
though we each, in turn,
walk the long white hall
into gray
into black
into nowhere known.

As We Come, As We Go

At the edge of winter
in crisp early March
a dull thud of numbness
delays joy and sadness
that will make us weep.

In the flow of life
every aspect bears its opposite.
Between extremes
there's the balance of peace
or peace
in the realization of balance.

With the warm blanket of knowledge
is the freezing cold of truth.
We are greeted with tears
as we come into this world
and tears as we go out.

The Wells

The wall behind me:
catcher of books, lebkuchen tins,
manuscripts, journals, pens,
an alien holding a remote,
a hand-tooled case made in prison,
a rabbit whose head opens to reveal
a chamber of butterflies,
gifts from the now gone,
baskets my father made
holding staples, clips and tape,
a Magritte print of water
against the reality of sea.
Albums:
flash records of seconds
over a lifetime,
a collage of femininity and belief,
a grandson with a foreign smile,
a patient, now dead,
fittingly against a sunset,
an 80's hug goodbye,
a daughter with fairy wings.

I embrace what is gone,
or is it what changes?
I reach out to touch the wells, whales, wails...
of my life.
I grasp only air
but hear rumors of angels.

Grasp

I would be anywhere
there is greenery and a body of water
anywhere not concrete
but fluid as the moment
solid as breath
peaceful as a sigh on the breeze.

I hang on to the world
with Spanish moss.

Selected Poems from

Finding Reality in Myth: Travels with Belinda

Chiron Review Press
Winner of the 1995
Chiron Review Chapbook Contest

Sun Rite / Other Ways

Close to the Sun Temple
depicting one thousand ways
to copulate
on the shore at Konarak
I was flattered
only white woman at sunrise
was given tea
a seat
a blanket.
I knew something
would happen
then men and women
went down on their knees
before me
as if before god.
They touched their foreheads
to the sand
in total adulation.
I trembled.
They faced the sun though
over the ocean
not me.
I was behind them.
It was the sun they loved.
Me,
they were mooning.

Then they went out
in their boats to fish
and made love to the sea.

Youth

A little boy balances
a basket on his head.
It's twice as wide as his waist
as thick as his head.
I cannot see his load.

He walks with such grace
perhaps it's peanut shells
or feathers or maybe food
something so badly needed
his happiness buoys him up.

But I must remember
I am a tourist.
The boy is young.
He is in his home.
Perhaps he has no burdens at all.

Priest

Looking back
at the photo I took
at the Krishna temple
I see what I hadn't seen.
The Priest is looking up
from his duties
with kind, sad eyes.
I see he is a good man.

He knows I desecrate
his temple
but he understands
I don't know that.

Not to Violate the Mind with Reason

I did not go inside
the most holy of Hindu temples
with my Indian in-laws.
I stood on the overlook
where I could see.

I dared not try
to connect the gods
with their temples
which are layered
and stacked in piles
like the cow dung cakes
offered within.

I dared not guess why
in the streets
the lonely cows roam
holy but starving

or why every sandal
is leather.

Snake Charmer

A dark Delhi turbaned boy
plays his wooden flute song.
His snake rises
only two inches
above the shallow wicker.
Perhaps it is sick
or the wrong sex
or it isn't its song.

He takes the snake
from the basket.
It rises eight inches
from the ground
but no further
and it doesn't sway.

The boy is in puberty.
Perhaps one day
his snake will learn
or perhaps his snake
is teaching him
and one day
the boy will learn.

Karnatik Classical: Thyagaraja Krithis

The Indian man parts his lips.
He is garbling.
He is humming.
He is ah-ing,
licking the air
passionately.

The music is hard.
His fingers stiffen.
A woman dances with her long neck.
He begins to dance with his.

The unknown tongue
says everything
as in the beginning
of all creation.

Sitar, voice and dance
become one.
Bare feet burn
until a string breaks,
a voice cracks,
the dance stops.

But nothing is ever the same.
The creation goes on
to become something else
then something else again

until
5,000 years later
an American in Germany
projects its profundity
too simply

and all you can think of
is sex.

Classical Indian Explanation: Music

Past the hippies
past Ravi Shankar
eons before
when the first Asian snake
came alive
stiffened with sound
through some empty shell
some hollow wood
some emptiness.

The snake
was not so much charmed
as listening intently
to the accidental flute,
to that which he knew
must be female,
its empty insides
calling him
with breath music

and he joined in
for awhile
finding a range of sounds
he'd never heard
then peace

and a new religion
practiced in places
where snakes are holy
and music
is written in his tongue.

My Name Is

Mary Subramanian
not Subraman.
I cut it short for Americans
who tongue-trip over names
longer than Smith or Jones.

Subramanian is a Hindu god,
son of Shiva and Pavoriti.
I went to his temple in Palini, India
where his priests blessed me
and dotted my head with kum-kum.

And Mary, of course, was the mother of Jesus.
Now you know my connection
to the gods—
you may call me Belinda
(my middle name, which is not holy)
or Bunny, a nickname,
which is quite a different story.

Selected Poems from

The Innocents

with Lyn Lifshin

Buzzard's Roost Press, 1991

The Accidental Elephant

Let's say you're traveling in India
and an elephant in a Hindu temple
salutes you with his trunk.
You notice the designs and paintings
on his forehead and body
and move in closer for a look.
The elephant wraps his trunk around you.
He likes you.

Hindus crowd around to see the white boy
blessed by Ganesh, a favorite god of good luck.
Let's say they begin to see you
as a reincarnation of Ganesh,
put garlands around your neck,
and bring you food, especially butter and limes.

Let's say you enjoy the attention,
the smiling admiring faces.
Then through an interpreter
you hear their prayers and pleas.
You learn they want their dying to be made healthy,
their destitute to be made wealthy,
their crippled to walk, their mute to talk.

Let's say you're inclined to give
the Sermon on the Mount and bless them with platitudes.
You even practice healings but none of them work.
So you learn magic and wow them with tricks,
enough so they bring you even more flowers, butter and limes
and their hard earned precious few rupees.

You accept them and bless them again.
They seem to be happy.
But you are not.
You live with an elephant.
You are god-like.
You are a liar.

Hell

I know about Hell. It is a gas station toilet inside a 4' by 4' room. The walls are painted yellow and the lighting is dim so all the world is a glowing stink.

Of course the plumbing is clogged. The toilet and sink overflow onto the floor. As time goes on the level rises to your knees, your waist, your elbows, your head. And yes, it swallows your head. Yellow and brown take your consciousness for a while. But you cannot die. You will be reincarnated into a baby's body on earth. You will be born to a low-class family with no morals. You will be beaten and molested. You will grow up believing there is no love in the world, and if you want something you just take it.

Somewhere down the road you will use guns. You will kill a few people who get in your way. You will be caught and sent to prison. You will almost like it because everything you need is there. It's the closest thing to love you've ever known. If only the doors didn't lock you'd be happy. You settle in for a long stay, trying to forget the death sentence.

But it comes around. They inject you with a poisonous drug and you lose consciousness for a while. You awake in a tiny room just big enough for a toilet, a sink and a tiny bed, as if you could rest there. The plumbing is clogged.

The walls are painted yellow and the lighting is dim so all the world is a glowing stink.

Concerted Efforts: Mainz Cathedral

We arrived early, for the concert, to standing room only. So we picked a comfortable pillar to lean against, you on one side, me on the other, with two strangers between us. Waiting for the music, we looked around and listened. We were too far away to hear what people were saying individually and the people close to us weren't talking. So we observed other people with things to say. We watched their mouths, faces and eyes.

Later we mentioned what we saw. We saw some of the same things, people. There was a woman with her hair all combed to the same side in a heavy pigtail, with a chiseled chin and hooked nose who was immensely proud of herself. She was an intrusion on everyone's sight. So we saw her.

When the concert began, at an angle I couldn't see, you noticed an old man who kept his eyes closed but was attentive to the music. He rocked his head and tapped his fingers. Perhaps he saw rapture with his eyes closed or could not bear to see such angelic sound coming from mere humans.

In front of you and to my side were two elderly ladies, at least in their eighties, each wearing one glove. I was touched, imagined they shared a pair. You didn't see this.

Near the end of the music, I was almost torn apart when a woman, near one hundred, was wheeled in by a woman in her sixties. She was probably her daughter. In any case, the younger dearly loved the elder. She kneeled beside her, stroked her face and caressed her head in a most tender manner. She was acutely aware the woman was dying.

Later, I told you about it. I thought you might have seen them. But you said nothing. Maybe you didn't hear. Or maybe you had your eyes closed and only saw the music.

Everything about France but the French

Leaning over Notre Dame Cathedral,
a double take with gargoyles
in overcast October
ten long-haired years ago,
I can only remember the tingles
of dreams and two hundred uneven
steps up and bumping my head
on the great bell when chosen
to demonstrate its sound quality
and holding back the screams, tears and curses
as the dull thud of my head
made bad music in Paris.
Later we ordered "two rooms full of wine"
when we had meant "glasses."
The Frenchman, being Turkish, was kind.

I remember the disappointing Mona Lisa
poking quiet fun eternally
to tourists, the snatching
of my jacket by women pushing
a baby carriage,
the descent from Notre Dame
to the woman serving transparent ham
in cement rolls
slowly and grudgingly
then shoving a tip dish at us
and the dark Sacred Heart on the hill
where artists believe away their lives.

No matter how many Americans
have made it home
millions have died there
having pissed and puked in bidets
having fallen for the gargoyles of night
the aura of myth
and the tingle of dreams.

The Growing Up Dream

I am five.
My grandmother
smells like polka dots
as she spits something
brown into the fire
of a cast iron stove.

She sews
and lies
because her warlock
won't allow it
but she has powers too.
Her false teeth
soaking in a clear glass
keep me at a distance.
I cannot overcome
their power
of disgust.

The little imp
who stays with us
eats raw bacon
pees on flowers
and disappears in the woods
to mislead me.

After a while
we're in a clearing
and there's a house
not of gingerbread
with an old witch

but a two-story shack
with an old man
whittling a cane
on its rotting front porch.
It hails crab apples
and the cane becomes a snake
which chases me
for many years.

Then finally I stop
and make peace
with the snake.
That day I buy and wear
a polka-dot dress
and smell like a woman.

Near the End: A Found Poem

Do you know the story on film
called *The Incredible Shrinking Man*?
He has a mysterious mishap
at the beach—
a cloud wafts over him.
He begins to grow smaller and smaller.
At last he is simply
a kind of one-celled organism.
He is invisible
but he speaks out in a sort of bliss.
He is neither more or less.
He is.
Everything is.
He knows finally that everything
is important and also
not important.
He is alive.
All that surrounds him is alive.
There is no death.

And so this morning in bed
I thought of this.
All night I dreamed a wild sort
of serial dream—
women of all sorts in it.
My dream was sluiced with mountain mist,
with salt spray
and lovely soughing breezes.
My eyeballs aflutter—
my cock straight up.
My electric blanket a baby blanket
and a tingling shroud too.

Selected Poems from

The Jesuit Poems

with Lyn Lifshin
Implosion Press, 1989

He Worships Women

Everywhere he sees
a goddess and
only her vision
gets him off.

At night he's at one
with his bed.
It drinks him in.

Womanhood rubs raw
his priesthood
like 80 lady poets
with long hair,
waitresses,
meter maids,
novices to his calling.

He sees that nuns have a lot
and Mother Superior is.

Sex for a Priest Is Tough

Angels will make him feel
he's sinned
and the demons will give him Guilt.
Together they make everything
in his day slide.
When he reaches up
to grasp Joy
he automatically slides back.
The forces make him feel
like putting the brakes
on orgasm
like it was some wild horse
he couldn't ride.

Wholly Men

They write wanting
wanting to know
about her breasts
if they are hard and boney
full and round.
They want them both ways
and at once.
They want to know
if she shaves her legs
and other places.
They want a souvenir,
send hundreds of dollars
for intimate garments
she has worn.
She fills their orders
with books.
They want something more.
They say perhaps
she didn't understand.
Again she sends them
books.
Perhaps they didn't
understand.

Fan

He has written her
many warm letters.
He's bought all her books
and phones her.
Once late at night
he wrote her name
in the snow
on her windshield.
It was the only time
she'd seen him
but she knew
his hands were cold.

Selected Poems from

Skin Divers

with Lyn Lifshin

Krax Publications, 1988

Water

You speak of whale water
like a reborn sailor
with Cornish eyes
full of a wet dream.

I grew up on well water,
the wholesome underground.
The sea was a yearly visit
a moving picture
that overwhelmed me.
I always came back
to what bodies need
the purest source.
Will you ever love the subtle,
my little sighs
or the wetness between my thighs?
I'm no ocean sailor.
I'm water you dig for.

Date Rape

First date,
he swings the car off the road,
says he has something for her,
the movie can wait.

Like a bank
hoping to earn interest
he offers her money.
She withdraws.

Then he tries inserting himself
like a coin
into a vending machine
wanting to bang impatiently
for the candy.

In the end
he pries her open
like a plumber
unclogging his pipes

then asks her
if she loves him.

Zen Sex

I am cycling
through the woods.
In heat, I unbutton
my blouse,
notice some daises
waving
pick 3 to ride
in my buttonhole.

We all cycle together.

I grow wet.
The bark on the trees
grows hard.

Selected Poems from

He Dreams His Playmate

Ghost Dance, Book #42, 1987

His First Door

The young solicitor
was nervous,
wanted
badly to be
somewhere else
yet lingered.

I thought perhaps
some womanly charm
showed through,
unsettled him.

It was only later
I noticed
my hair stuck out
each side
like wings,
not of angels
but of something evil
swooping in...
something that could capture
a salesman.

This Drink

takes me back
to Germany
and a Folkfest
in a beer tent
with an 80 year old man
saying
“You’re so slim”
and moving his hands,
shaping the air into
an hourglass
because I’d lost 5 lbs
that week starving
accidentally for attention
like this
with my husband
beside me
who loves me
because others do.

Selected Poems from

Eye of the Beast

Vergin' Press, 1986

Tells No One

This child
misses school
for lack of clothes.
It's winter.
A fire is in
the tent
she stays close to...
She tells no one
where she lives
but describes a home
normal, unimposing,
average, hoping
no one will notice
newspaper patches
in her shoes,
holes in her clothes
she covers with
a 4th-hand sweater.
Sometimes her mother
is gone for days
but she knows to fetch
firewood from fallen branches
and water from gas station
restrooms in plastic milk jugs,
to ask for spare change
in the far end of town.

She's eight years old
and Indian.

You turn you head
when you see her
but occasionally a man
touches her body
for the price
of a warm meal,
a night's sleep
in an ordinary house
like she dreams of.

The Trap

The little mouse
comes out
views the trap
thinks how he can
get at the cheese
without at least
bruising his tail.
He giggles
a little mouse giggle.
The mouse is a mechanic.
He takes the trap apart
little screw by little wire
for a long mouse time
then grabs the cheese
and runs
but is found dead
later anyway
from poisoned cheese.

Ceremony

Soldiers march in
like bad actors
in a movie
I can't believe
sit in front of
a giant flag
fluttering
from a wind machine.

Wives are asked
to stand
and be recognized
hop up and down
like puppets on chains.

A General reads
from a comic book
on pride
and conquering
like a cock
crowing for his mate.

Hail to glorious battle
where promotions are faster
and death is a holiday
that never ends,
an endless leave,
permanent R and R.

and the wife
gets a poker chip
stamped BRAVE
in a velvet lined box
like a coffin
and a flag
that no longer waves.

Ignorance Is Not Bliss

"You don't know what you've done," he says.

The old man breaks a door
says it's our fault
not his
that he can't break out
and be wonderful.

The children cry.
They weren't missed.
They were hit
by many words.

The old man plays
with the broken pieces,
thinks he can patch the door
and we'll forget.
He says it's enough
it wasn't our teeth
or our bones.

The old man says
we've ruined his evening
points his finger
like a gun
dares us to do it again.

The old man stills plays
with the pieces.
We want to do what he says.
We don't want to die
of finger wounds
or shattered bones but
we don't know what we've done.

Selected Poems from

Fighting Woman

Planet Detroit Chapbooks, 1986

The Unlikely Professor

is a serious poet
playing at teaching
what he believes
cannot be taught.

He's a sexy sexagenarian
keeps a centerfold layout
in his open book
as he teaches
gets hot on the subject
(sizes up the girls
in class
imagines them
spread out,
stapled).
The students admire
his smile, his lines,
his enthusiasm
and his strong, tall
podium
which hides his firm
disbelief.

If You Insist on Truth

Lowered in your arms
I have laid plans
for happiness.
Intense eternities
are etched.
I have swallowed you
whole and easily
as a dying metaphor.

It is a bad time to tell me
what I have ingested
is poisonous.
It is a bad time to tell me
you are terminal
and married
and good night
means
only one.

Late Night
in the Psyche Ward

Lummox Press
Red Book series #37, 2001

Names and dates were changed to protect the innocent, and the guilty.

Dedicated to all those, who even once,
thought they were "crazy."

August 1

From the outside

my job may look easy.
What could be so stressful?
Never mind no one I work with makes sense
and I cannot sleep at night.
There's a cemetery
by the psych hospital
with only the width
of a two lane road
between them.
Every night from the third floor
I look down on the past
and the future.

Every night
I turn into work.
I drive myself
between the insane
and the dead.

August 4

Peter tells me what's missing

in his life is
"clarity of psycho insight,
integrated entity,
singularity of thought train,
emotional isometric order,
systematic equational interlude,
local creation,

atomization, singularization,
a natural Gibraltar,
a mother and a nuclear family image,

a mother."

August 5

Peter orders dinner

in a note stating,
"Please give moral character of *Gunsmoke* and *High Noon*
in my supper meal.
Give Bible character lessons of *God's Little Acre*
in my supper meal.
Give love and security of *Leave It to Beaver*
in my supper meal.
Give character of *My Three Sons*
in my supper meal.
Give simple love of John Boy from the *Waltons*
in my supper meal.
Give universal knowledge
in my supper meal

and coffee."

August 6

Peter's personal mandala

My greatest strength:
"Independence."
My greatest weakness:
"Chila Dahile Lama Sri."
What I would give my life for:
"Cash."
My greatest fear:
"Loneliness."
My greatest hope:
"*%#(!)."
My heroes:
"Kicotil one soup."
Three things I am not:
1. "Boastful."
2.
3.

August 28

Peter was gone when I came on duty.

Raul of Rio, Juan Multi.
I'll miss his late night pacing.
One night in the midst of mumbling
a secret language
he stopped, looked at me and said,
"The circumference of the earth
is 500,000 miles. Is that right?

"Well, Peter, I don't have those figures
on the top of my head."

"I don't either, he says
and continues pacing.

I'll miss those notes he gave
to make contact with the outside world.
One was a sample decoding
of his private language called "Forward XXX."
It read:
85th birthday = Fortica Corpsa
osteoporosis = Demi Prec
leukemia = Yata-detae
dendrite decay = formented

He was quieter the days before he left.
But when he talked it was still
word salad or incoherent.
Perhaps staff took quieter for better.
They released him to a homeless shelter.
He hates shelters.

He likes wide-open spaces
where he can smoke
whenever he can find a cigarette,
where he can walk naked unrestricted
until someone calls the police
and they bring him back here
which starts the cycle
all over again.

September 5

Peter is back after only eight days.

He was caught directing traffic, naked,
claiming to be Charlie Manson and Hitler.
He's sunburned, scratched up.
His feet are cracked and cut
from walking barefoot.
His voice is garbled, sounds like he's barking
with a mouth full of gravel.
But he continues dropping lists at the desk.
Some lists tell us who he is: "a homosexual and a lesbian
and Zar governor of Andromeda Strain..."
Some tell us diseases he wants cured: "Soviet's tongue,
Heineken's turmoil, defecation rot..."
Other lists tell us who he wants
at his "ordination breakfast"
where "wurlitzer coffee" is to be served.
He wants Clinton, Popeye, Queen of England,
Daffy Duck, Mortimer Snerd, King Tut...
In the past he's told me
he sold dope to Jerry Garcia,
shot up with Grace Slick.
Said he likes "combo shotgun"
and rattled off a list of drugs.
He showed me "tracks" on his arm.
But I didn't see much, two or three red dots.
And I just got his toxicology screen results.
Negative for all drugs.
His problem is his brain.
Schizophrenic for 50 years.

He's basically harmless.
Claims to be God-fearing
and—God.

September 6

Tonight I admitted Ching-Lee,

an Asian lady with broken English
and paranoid schizophrenia.
She sat at a table and wrote
frantically—a letter
to Mr. Bell Clean-tun, our president,
who will help her
and who will one day be king.
On the basis of this letter
which I put into her files
the Dr. is considering mania
as an alternative diagnosis.
In her letter she states several times
that she can do anything,
that she can change the constitution,
help Mr. Clean-tun, etc.
She had been calling the FBI
and Secret Service trying to get the wife
of her ex-husband arrested because,
"He still love me in his heart place.
He can no be with another woman."
But her record states he denies
ever having been married to her.
Perhaps she was with him in Korea
as she says and he brought her to the States
where he dumped her
but blaming doesn't cure
and sickness isn't handed out like candy.

Like the wife of T.S. Eliot
she sings the praises of a man
who would commit her.
The same man who disowned her
and cut her from him bleeding
states, “I don’t want to see her.
I am happy now.”

September 10

Ethel comes to me, excitedly saying,

“Isn’t it amazing how a cat moves
and the pots I painted don’t.
But anything that moves
you have to feed.
And later the by-product comes out.
I wouldn’t mind feeding the pots
and seeing where they moved to each day.
I wouldn’t even mind
cleaning up pot shit.
But what if a pot didn’t like the cat
and flipped over on top of it?
Oh no! It could suffocate and die!”

“More likely,” I say, “the cat would
knock over the pot and break it.”

Ethel’s jaw drops.
“Oh wow, thanks.
That solves that problem.”

September 20

The night before last

Oscar came out of his room
every five minutes
and every five minutes we told him
it was late at night
and to go back to bed.
Each time he said,
"Go back to bed. Okay,"
and he went.
But his short term memory loss
kicked in and he immediately forgot.
He'd come right back out
and so on it went all night.

Last night we learned a trick.
If you put his shoes away
he won't come out
because he never leaves
without his shoes.
So all night long
he opened his door,
looked out, then closed it.
He couldn't leave.
He had no shoes.

October 10

Clara is better.

Her imaginary spiders are dead
and she is no longer upset
with her imaginary daughter.
She is now teaching her how
to make enchiladas.

November 5

Rueben couldn't sleep.

He kept wanting to talk about sex.
He asked me, "Why do I have to
get rid of women
as soon as I have sex with them?"
I tried to ignore images of women's bodies
that have been found in the desert lately
and said, "Maybe it's hard for you to trust, etc...."
My observation time with him was short.
I told him, "Good luck.
I hope I don't see you again
...except in K-Mart or something"
while the words "getting rid of women"
echoed in the pit of my stomach.

December 4

At 3:30 a.m.,

Kim, another lady with a Korean accent
tells me the story
of the evening she was brought here.
She said she was "taking medicine"
because she was very upset and angry
over what someone had said to her.
She understands little English
so she dialed "O" on the telephone
looking for information.
She asked the operator
what "asshole" meant.
The operator hung up.
She called her again and asked her to please
talk to her, that she was taking medicine
and asked again, "What does asshole mean?"
The operator apparently had the call traced.
At some point the police showed up
and Kim was frightened as well as angry.
Many pills were on the table.
She violently brushed them to the floor
and began throwing things at the police.
She doesn't understand why she is here.
She tells me to please tell
her story to the doctor
so he will let her go.

December 15

Johnnie comes out of his room at 2:30 a.m.

with orange food stains and rice
stuck around his mouth,
mutters something in Spanish
and kisses my hand.
I graciously accept, smiling
silently marking my hand for a wash
in the near future.
Then I remind him
that my Spanish is little,
that I'm so sorry.
He pulls out his little English for me
and says, "I am one man,
you are one lady,"
then falls back into Spanish.
I do not know if it's his way
of proposing a rendezvous
or he's just getting his labels straight.
My Hispanic tech is on break.
I tell him someone will translate
for us in a few minutes.
But he loses interest.
That would make two men and one lady.
That's not what he had in mind.

January 6

My tech tells me

back when he did all the street drugs
he knew Richard Ramirez,
the serial killer.
They were from the same barrio.
He also knew a necrophiliac
who worked in a morgue
on the night shift.
He "did" all the dead women
who came in.
All ages, shapes and colors
turned him on.
When he saw a good looking live women
he'd say, "I wouldn't mind
having her dead."

My tech before this one
said he was in a gang
from ages 14-19,
killed some people,
spent some time in jail.
Left the gang life
when his brother was killed.

Maybe it's true
that people who work in psych
are all ex-wackos themselves,
which begs a question
I don't care to answer.

February 2

Lolly, a homeless lady and 79

came in last night.
She believes Hitler is out to get her.
She insists she is isn't a patient,
that she was kidnapped.
She refuses food, vital signs, medications,
every aspect of treatment.
She even refuses to go to her room.
She sits upright all day and night
in a lounge chair in the day room.
Her only known history is from records
of previous admissions
in which she also refused everything,
including a physical.
She's old enough to have been affected
directly by Hitler's reign of terror.
But she has a Texas accent.
Her name is not Jewish or German
and she's also threatened by the Coke machine.

Peter, a homeless man,
who has been admitted three times in four months,
thinks he's Hitler...
Although it sounds like a disaster
waiting to happen
each is too internally stimulated
to be aware of the other.
Side by side horrors play out
behind the concentration walls of their minds.

We give them a warm dry place, free food
and respect, even when they refuse,
even when they lash out.
They are safe
from themselves,
from each other,
from us.

February 10

Commotion at the change of shift

involved a doctor checking out
one of our geriatric patients
for "labor pains."
She was seven months pregnant
so it was possible.
Since we're a mental hospital
we aren't equipped to deliver babies
so the doctor called the medical hospital next door.
Labor and delivery didn't believe us.
"What, a geriatric patient in labor?"
"Well yes, she's an overflow from another unit.
She's 46, bipolar with psychotic features.

So we wheel her through the tunnel
that joins the two hospitals.
She calls the tech who is younger than her, Daddy,
and at the same time flirts with him
between pains.
Other than wanting sex all the time
and being slow witted
she had seemed okay to me.
Then she had to go and tell us
she'd been a car and a glass
in previous lives. Hmmm...
Things that don't move, feel or give birth.

Turns out it was “false labor,”
non-productive pains.
She’s back with us
resting with her baby still inside
sharing her anti-psychotics,
her cigarettes,
her men,
her search for daddy.

February 11

Raymond speaks rapidly

and with authority
and pretense at genius,
claims he was once autistic
and the movie *Rain Man*
was about him.
"Rain-man" he says
"equals Ray-mond."
Hmmm.
But I say, "Autistic people
often never speak."
"I wouldn't say shit if my mouth
was full of it," he answers.
Then to "prove" his skills
he rapidly fires astronomical equations.
Most likely bullshit
but the speed was impressive.
So my charge nurse figures up
how many days it takes
for one million seconds to pass
and our false genius is way off.
His defense is, "There's a factor
you didn't figure in.
God rewound his wrist watch
and there was a lapse of time."
Un huh!
Then he goes on about being a pilot
in an undercover operation,
how he jumped from helicopters without a parachute,
how Boeing prized him so much
they pay him $8,000 a year for life

just because they like him.
He has proof he says.
But the paper he shows
is a W2 form from an insurance company
with an “X” marked for sick pay.
Un huh. That’s believable.
On and on he talks.
I want to turn away
but he’s known to get violent if he’s ignored.
Then my charge nurse decides to save me
and sends me on a bogus mission
with a wink of an eye.
Raymond lets me go “this time”
because “work is important”
but “we’ll talk later”
and he winks too.

February 12

So Raymond continues imparting wisdom...

"Most people are on
an itty bitty pity potty committee."

"Do you know what the most stolen item
at Walgreens, K-Mart and Walmart is?
Preparation H.
Most people are assholes
and I guess they itch."

"Do you know I've written 79 books
all under different pseudonyms.
I wrote *The Magic of Believing*
by Claude M. Bristol
and *Seekers of Wisdom*
by John Fire LameDeer.
I'm part Sioux.
My grandmother was Mini Ha,
second daughter of Sitting Bull,
Crazy Horse's sister.
So do you know what that makes me?"

(I wonder for a millisecond if he's trying to tell me,
in code, that he thinks he's "crazy,"
but nah...)

I just look at him and say,
"Got me."

February 13

Gloria wants to call the police

and tell how she was kidnapped
and held captive here
(not remembering it was the police
who brought her in).
She also feels we keep her family
from visiting her.
She says they come to the door and knock
but we won't let them in.
(Truth is they refuse to see her.)
She says, "If only they could be
picked up in a van and driven by here,
I could see them. I could at least wave
out the window."
I realize her vast loneliness.
She looks to me as an authority
who can make anything happen.
She asks, "Will you write it down
that I can see my family?"
I pause a minute
then write, "Gloria may see
her family if they come to the hospital"
and I sign my name and title.
She clutches it and smiles
and says, "Oh thank you.
Maybe I can sleep now."

February 25

It's a quiet night.

Only five patients
for two nurses.
It's a great time
to catch up on reading.
I've brought a poetry book,
a design motif book,
a ceramics magazine
and various expensive junk catalogs
that I enjoy seeing before tossing.
I peruse these items
in reverse order
saving the best for last.
It is at this time
that my 25 year old "boss"
turns the radio on.
A heavy metal song blares,
"I'm on the highway to hell."
I sneak a hand under my hair
and plug my ear with a finger.
But I can't concentrate.
He thinks the radio isn't loud.
I want to keep
a good working relationship.
I try to keep reading.
I want to keep busy.
It's 2 a.m. Stillness becomes sleep.
But I've stopped reading.

I've stopped to write this.
I've stopped writing...

February 26

Lady who wears a wig

to protect her two-way brain...
Lady who believes she has $10,000,000,000
in a London bank...
Lady who believes her neighbors
zapped her house with rays
that made her appliances and clocks
go haywire...
Lady who knows the President,
who has the power to make him King...
Lady who believes astral spirits molest her
and want to steal her soul...
Lady who sees spiders everywhere
and is serenaded by mice...

These are just a few of my ladies,
gems of despair
hanging on to fiction,
choking the awful truth
they can't bear,
stuck in a nether world somewhere.

March 4

He calls himself a silly name,

something like Juan Zipadeedoo Zipadeeday.
He says he's Apache,
however, he speaks only Spanish.
I've "lived" with him five nights a week
for two months now.
Mostly he's sweet, colors little pictures
like he's in kindergarten, although he's 75.
Sometimes he acts up like a child
having a tantrum, shouts and throws things.
Then we have to give him medication
for severe agititation.
He calls me "Merry Christmas"
and insists on kissing my hand.
For all intents and purposes
he is Juan Zipadeedoo Zipadeeday,
until tonight.
For some reason administration
changed his name to John Doe,
probably to extend his stay
since no claims him.
He has nowhere to go.
He owns nothing
and now,
he has no name.

March 10

Our unit has nine tonight

with one L.O.S. meaning "Line of Sight"
but really meaning "Line of Sleep."
A tech is required to sit in front
of a patient's door all night,
doing nothing but watching.
Techs love this duty.
They catch up on sleep
while the R.N does regular tech duties
as well as her own.

The nurse helping me tonight
keeps dropping off to sleep too.
She mumbles and snorts
as if in distress.
I ask her if she's all right.
"I was having a nightmare.
I dreamed I was in a mental hospital.
Nothing made sense."

Meanwhile, Peter, who thinks he's a girl, wakes up
wanting juice with milk
and leaves this word of wisdom:
"There's an old Chicano saying
that if a girl doesn't like you
another man will tell her parents."
Then he runs to his room
and slams the door.

March 12

I've been listening to a nurse

who likes soap operas and romance novels,
who's playing country music
at 3 a.m. in the psych ward
while I wish to read Carl Sagan
in silence
in between interruptions
from the insane.
I find I am irritated
by the mere mouthings
of a shallow soul who aspires
to pray for the poor dears
in between talk shows
on her days off.
I am irritated
that I'm irritated,
feel I should have the patience of Job
on my job.

I'm tired. My head aches
from trying to make sense
of the neuron explosions
in some of these brains.
Tonight
there were no new displays
of psychosis.
They all slept, making time go by
like molasses sliding down a mountain side,
sunlight reaching for Pluto.

And I'm just a key away from coffee
locked in an iron vault...
the key in the pocket of a man
who believes he's God
and he's nowhere to be seen.

March 13

"Do you believe in angels?"

my charge nurse asks.

"I don't know," I say.
"Reason tells me no.
Romance tells me yes."

As if blanking out
half my answer he asks,
"Do you think everything
revolves around reason?"

Sensing his Catholic dogma
unchallenged noticeably
by thought, I say,
"Obviously not. We hardly ever
believe anything,
see anything
or hear anything reasonable,
especially here."

Silence.

Silence is golden.

April 2

My nurse partner and I

have threatened for months
to stop at a bar
on the way home
and have a beer together.
Finally a group of six nurses and techs
stop by the infamous bar
at 7:45 a.m. on a Saturday.
We tell ourselves
it's our weekend
and equal to everyone else's
Friday night.
But we're a little self-conscious.
Very soon we notice
a much larger group of nurses
from another hospital
wearing tell-tale scrubs
drinking margaritas.
I feel less sinister,
less repressed by the Baptist ideals
of my youth
and we order another beer.
I realize this is an easy ritual
for night shift workers.
No one knows we're nurses.
Our nametags are in our pockets.
We're wearing street clothes
as required in psych.
No one knows we're nurses
concerned with substance abuse
and mental pain.

We look like loose chicks
starting way too early.

At 10:00 a.m. as we leave
a group of young men is coming in.
We say to them giggling,
"We can't believe
people drink this early!"
They look amused, cockeyed
and go in to socialize and drink
with a different excuse.

April 3

“Did you hear the news?”

they asked me when I came in.
“Did you hear there was a little boy
run over by his mother
and killed instantly?
That was Jack’s little boy.”
Jack is a nurse on our floor
and of course he’d gone home.
We expressed our horror and disbelief.
John said we’d say a prayer for him.
Before I knew it we were holding hands
in a circle
and a few words were said.
The words were self-conscious
to a non-proven entity.
They couldn’t have helped Jack.
It couldn’t have helped us.
But it brought us closer
for a few seconds.
I believed in the caring.

April 5

Gloria is back in the psych ward

tied up in a posey vest
because she's a fall risk
and at age 76
a fall could cripple her.
She's also disoriented, stumbles,
and mumbles incoherently.
I feel for her.
She came in with bruises
all over her body.
Someone had abused her.
At least we walk her around,
talk nicely to her,
feed her, give her things to do,
keep her clean and calm her
when she flails about and screams,
stuck in the middle of a nightmare.
But she doesn't understand the vest.
She says she doesn't want it.
People will think she's crazy.

April 6

I work in a mental institution

all night long
five days a week.
I have to sleep in the daylight. Alone.
I get up...alone...in the afternoon
as the light is falling,
feeling drained.

On weekends I try to sleep with my partner.
My body is confused and anguished on Saturdays,
not knowing how to sleep at night anymore.
Sundays are with my daughters,
then his mother,
almost never a day for myself
or just to relax.

Mondays I'm up 24 hours
because I can't sleep in the day
after having slept Sunday night.
Then I go back to work
Monday night...all night long
and so on.

Yet it's exciting being a psych nurse
and I'm making four times the salary
I ever did.

But it's a grind too.

One I would give up
in a heartbeat
if I won the lottery.
Failing that
part time would be enough
and a loving man
who would not want to see me stressed
if he could help it,
who would have a woman with time
to love him properly.

I want to enjoy my life.
I want to soar
with my heart.

April 8

Everyone is sleeping now

though last night six people were raving.
One telling me the devil is real
and trying to destroy him.
One in a posey vest straining to get up
to buy tomatoes.
One who says she's President of the U.S.A.,
Canada, Brazil and Japan.
One who thinks everyone's out to rape her,
who questions the Dr's orders for a urine sample
saying we only want to drink her liquid gold.
You get the picture.

Management has been telling us
they've been losing a million dollars
every six months
and they're closing the floor,
laying some of us off.
Tomorrow appears to be the day.

I'll miss this exclusive, crazy club.
Where else will a trash can be launched at you
by a man who wants to know, goddamnit,
what ship he's on.
I'll especially miss the schizophrenics
and serial killers.
Life here doesn't yawn.
It's sick, insane, wearing
but never boring.

I’ve never done LSD.
But I’ve done this.

April 9

My last morning in geriatric psych

My last morning in geriatric psych
Kitty told me, “We’re a lot alike.
We’re both left-handed and have red hair.
Well, I used to have red hair.”
She also told me it was her birthday.
I checked it out to make sure.
No telling what someone will tell you
in a place like this.
Sure enough, it was her birthday. 77 years old.
I checked to see if she needed any lotion,
slipper socks or any little thing
we could supply.
I had to act fast because
I was getting ready to leave.
She didn’t need any thing I could offer
but a few minutes later
she came to the nurse’s desk and asked,
“I hate to beg, but do you have today’s paper?”
Ah hah, maybe I could find her one.
I asked the nurses and techs
who were going to relieve us.
A tech had the paper
and graciously offered it.
She took it and said,
“Not much good happens in the world
but there’s still Doonesbury.”
She carefully tore out her favorite comic strip
and handed the paper back saying,
“Thank you. I can tell
it’s going to be

a great day!"

And I knew
I'd made her happy.

April 10

Many get better here

Many get better here.
Many don't.
I can't give you an ending,
a final conclusive thought.
Even with one foot out the door
one foot is still
amidst the extravagantly ill,
the mundanely troubled.
The down part of life
is microscoped in my face.
Guilt, sorrow, mangled love,
tortured interiors, underbelly of fear,
explosive thinking, disappearing selves...
No one comes here wearing a smile.
Everyone leaving does.

Notes of a Human Warehouse Engineer

Liquid Paper Press, 1998

First Prize winner
1998 Nerve Cowboy Chapbook Contest

These poems chronicle my eight month stint as a Certified Nurse Assistant in a nursing home in the border town of El Paso, Texas. I gained insight into what it is like to be in the minority in this country. In my case it was being an "anglo" among a majority of Spanish-speaking people of Mexican heritage. But the most important insight I gained was into the widespread and growing practice of warehousing our elders.

Belinda Subraman, AKA Mary Subramanian

For Bill and Veronica
and for all those who care for the elderly
with kindness and respect.

CNA Clinical December 16-21

The first two nights
I had a partner.
Our resident was unable
to feed herself and we spoon
fed her pureed food.
She was unable to walk
and even a two-person transfer
from bed to wheelchair was
difficult.
We made a point to pat
her shoulders and look into
her eyes as we talked.
Soon she was holding our hands
and smiling.
In her moments of clarity
she told us she had had a good life,
that her husband was a good man.
Later she burst out singing.
I'm not sure if it was a song she knew
or if it was the moment
that moved her to sing,
"My heart is so filled with love,
I could die."

December 22

Mrs. Regalado sings softly in Spanish

to me and asks me if I like her song.
I tell her yes, I feel honored.
She begins to sing in English for me,
"Sweet, lovely, Mary, Mary."
And I love this 97 year old woman
who weighs no more than 60 pounds,
whose brittle legs no longer
bend at the knees,
whose bones creak when she moves,
who puts her arms around me
as I lift her from the bed to the wheelchair
and says "wheeeeee."

She asks me if I'll be here tomorrow
and when I tell her I will be gone for two days
she looks sad and asks where I will be for two weeks.
And I say, "Only two days, not weeks."
She beams and sighs relief.

December 24

Mrs. Rixford was told five days ago

that her daughter was coming for Christmas
and for five days she has sat
at the glass door waiting,
sometimes standing and gently
waving her hand for hours.

At dinner time
as I was giving room service
I found Mrs. Rixford
curled up in bed.
I talked to her
and encouraged her to eat.
Surprisingly, she did.
And she got back into bed.
And her daughter never came.

December 27

Mrs. Venable takes a long time to satisfy.

She has routines of hundreds of steps
which must be followed in order.
Turn left, right, push here, pull there,
put this here and that there and so on.
All the time she calls me "honey'"and "mother"
and I don't mind too much
so I let her hog my time
until I think I've pleased her
only to hear the next day
she has complained
and a social worker breathes down my neck
as if I had beat the woman.
Then I talk to the nurse on duty
who says she's a spoiled, rich Mexican woman
who's gotten aides fired for things
he knows they didn't do.
All I can think of is did I miss one of her
100 steps or get one out of order?

Later on she rings her bell twenty minutes
before I'm to go home.
Oh no. I go and see.
She wants to go to the bathroom,
one of her
100 step programs.
At first I lie and tell her
I will send someone, and leave.
But then I tell myself to be what it is
I think I am, and I go back
and try to learn the steps.

December 28

After dinner I took Mrs. Cunningham

to her room to put her to bed.
First I had to remove the chunks of food
from her fists.
“Let me take this away Mrs. C.
We don’t want you to sleep with crumbs.”
And Mrs. C. with a sly smile on her hundred
year old mouth says,
“I hadn’t planned on it.
I’ll be sleeping alone, thank you.”

December 29

Mrs. Garcia, as usual, shouted

in Spanish, she wanted to
make a phone call, she wanted
to go home, she did not want
to be here and other things
I could not understand.
Near 10 p.m. while making
final rounds for my shift
she was still yelling.
She reached out to me
as she does everyone,
for a hug and kiss.
I allowed it, hoping
it would soothe her
and I kissed her cheek.
But she clung to me in a death grip
and I had to peel her off
finger by finger, speaking gently.
I had not soothed her.
I had briefly thrown her an anchor
in a savage sea
and tore it away from her.
And she kept on yelling.

December 30

Mrs. Lehman spoke tonight.

For nine days I've seen her
sitting lifeless,
eyes off into space.
I thought I had learned
not to underestimate
the fire of life inside
even through agony, illness and old age
but while making rounds
to see if they were dry,
I asked Mrs. Lehman
as I asked everyone,
"Do you need anything?"
And she said, "I am very cold.
I think I'm catching a cold."
As I went to get her a blanket
I was beaming and told the nurse,
"Mrs. Lehman spoke!"
proud as if my baby had learned to talk.

January 12

Mrs. Lankford arrived today,

a beautiful woman with scrambled brains.
One minute she was reading
a Bible verse on the wall,
the next minute she was speaking
word salad of life review.
She doesn't know how to ride
in a wheelchair.
She drags her feet and grabs for the wall.
She feels her mind spinning.
She has to be fed
or she eats her napkin
and throws her food away.
Of course, she wears a diaper and a bib.
Mrs. Lankford arrived today,
already gone.

January 13

Mrs. Estrada is 98

and the only one who walks
without pushing a wheelchair
or using a cane.
She's on the go and hard to find.
She takes walks, visits with others,
has afternoon tea in the dining room.
After dinner she helps the aides
wheel her junior housemates
back to their rooms.
When you offer her help
she says, "No thanks, I'll do it.'

This lady will not slip away quietly,
lay down her ghost and leave us.
She will be found grasping the bed rails
trying to get up to live.

January 17

Mrs. Rios

is 500 pounds of anger
against " you no speak *espanol,*" me.
Nurse Bill tells her,
"We're in America, Spanish
is not a requirement, besides,
I don't speak Spanish either."
But it doesn't matter.
I'm merely a *gringa* to her,
convenient to abuse.
I and the other aides help her anyway.
Without us, she can't move.

January 27

Spanish I have learned so far:

Venga. Come here.
Acuesta me. Put me to bed.
Prende la luz. Turn on the light.
Apaga la luz. Turn off the light.
un savanna: a sheet
una coveha: a blanket
cama: bed
arriba: top
abajo: bottom
Esta bien? Is it okay?
Es bien. It's okay.
campana: call bell
pompis: rear end
papas: potatoes
sapeta: diaper
zapatos: shoes
limpio: clean
susio: dirty
mojado: wet
seca: dry
Lista? Ready?
Vamos. Let's go.
Yo estoy aprendiendo español. Mrs. Rios.
I am learning Spanish, Mrs. Rios.

January 28

Mrs. Clune died this afternoon.

She lay cold in her bed.
with the curtains drawn
while I dressed her roommate
who was going to dinner
with her family.
At first I was told
to dress her in the shower.
The nurse was afraid
her family would come in
and see the dead body
but I suggested the family
could wait in the sitting room
and I would bring her out
when she was ready.
Dilemma solved.
Mrs. Garcia would go out
for dinner
and her family would never know
she roomed with a corpse.

January 29

Tonight we found Mrs. Willy

wandering the halls
"looking for her little boy."
"How old are you, Mrs. Willy?"
I asked.
"86," she said.
"How old would your youngest son be now?"
"65."
"That's not a little boy is it?"
"No."
"Which of your sons is the only one living?"
"Howard."
"How old is he now?"
"71, I was 15 when I had him."
"He's not a little boy now, is he?"
"No, I was confused. But to me, he's my little boy.
You never stop worrying about your children out at night,
do you?"
"No, I guess not, Mrs. Willy."
And she took my hands and let me lead her back to bed.
And she said, "You're a mother, you understand."

February 3

Mrs. Herrara was sweet tonight.

"Please" and "thank you"
came out of her mouth
every time she rang.
No grunts, groans or insults as before.
Also, Mrs. Rios asked for me by name
instead of a Spanish girl.
She said, "Get Mary, she is tall."
Mrs. Sorenson would not go to bed
until I gave her a back rub.
"Mary is the best you know.
She's going to be a massage therapist,"
she tells others out in the hall.
Even the nurses asked,
"Why is it so peaceful?"
another aide said, "Oh, they're all high."

I don't know what came over everyone
but there was a full moon tonight
and Mary was tall.

February 4

Mrs. Hijar suddenly said in English

"I am God."
"You are God?"
"No," she answered,
my daddy is God."
"Oh, that's good. I would not
know what to say if I was in
the room with God."
And Mrs. Tigg, her roommate
added, "Me neither. Goddamn,
that was a close call."

February 19

Mrs. Garcia attacked me

while getting her dressed
for dinner,
pinched my arm so bad it bled,
hurt my breast
and just missed poking my eye out.
I called nurse Bill for help.
He kept her arms from striking
while I finished pulling her pants up.
Safely seated in her wheel chair
with her protective “lab buddy”
restraint,
she began sweet talking me in Spanish,
calling me little sister
and asking me to put her to bed
but I felt no sympathy
even though I knew
she was brought here because
no one could handle her
and it was my job to try.

February 20

Mrs. Garcia's new roommate,

Mrs. Fulladosa, curses
in Spanish, calls us all
dogs, bitches and whores,
spins around in her bed,
pokes her fingers up her rear
and eats her feces.
Mrs. Garcia has taken to calling
her roommate a dog, a bitch and a whore.
And they tell each other to shut up.
I've seen it over and over again.
Demented women do not make friends.

February 27

Mrs. Sorenson says she's tired

of staying up late
to catch the underwear thief.
She's hiding a pink nightie
under her pillow as bait.
The underwear thief comes
in the middle of the night
and depletes the supplies of old ladies
but if the thief takes
something blue
she will return it.
The underwear thief
doesn't like blue.

Mr. Flores offered me $4.00
(possibly all the money he had)
if I would sleep with him.

Mrs. Hijar says she was raped
and shot again in her wheelchair.

Mrs. Levelette says
she has a bedpan
in her vagina.

It was a normal night.

March 13

Mrs. Martin is back

from the hospital,
third time in three months.
This time the anesthetic
has demented her.
She had a phone dangling
from her bed.
She wanted to speak to Robert Lee.
The address book was on her night stand.
I looked for "Lee." No Lee.
"Sorry, I don't see Robert Lee."
"Robert E. Lee," she said.
Oh.

March 26

Mrs. Rios has 30 days to leave

the nursing home.
She has caused too much trouble
for too many
including calling the cops
with invented stories of abuse
and trying to throw herself
on the floor
while being transferred
just to get aides fired.
My learning Spanish did little
to appease her anger at my "angloness."
So, *Mi casa no es su casa, Señora Rios.*
Adios.

April 28

Finally got a dinner break at 9 p.m.

although I was using the time to sign two books
of ADL charts
when a disrespectful smart-ass
from laundry
probably on her 10th break
says to me,
"Y'all got any full barrels over there?"
"No, they're either off the floor or new ones."
"Well. I figure," she says
"if I can do my job you can do yours."
"What do you mean?"
"Well, if when those old people piss and shit
all over themselves and you go to get fresh linen
you want it to be there, don't ya?"
I just went on signing the books.
I could tell she had no idea how hard we worked,
the scope of what we did, or how much
all those great grandmothers and grandfathers
depended on us to care for them
with dignity and respect.
At least mentally, I slapped her face.
My training had taught me
to respect the ignorant and cruel alike,
not just the incontinent.

May 1

I knew Pearl for a while.

She used to sit in the hall
and tell everyone I was the best.
She was always glad to see me
and thanked me profusely.
And I was happy to help her.
I hope it was enough.

In her last few days
she was complaining that nobody cared.
In my rush, I did not reassure her.
Soon after, she was bedridden
and breathing rapidly.
While taking her pulse
she reached up and stroked my face.
She died within hours.
Little Pearl no more.
I had to be strong
but on the way home
nobody cared
if water leaked from my face.
And it did
for awhile.

May 19

Spanish

in a quiet monotone
sounds like this to me:
“um uh uh um mmm baño.”
So, I’ll take you to the bathroom.
Spanish
in a shrill excited tone
sounds like this to me:
“caw me caw yap yo caw baño.”
So, I’ll take you to the bathroom.

May 27

While trying to rescue

Mrs. Hijar
from sliding out of her chair
I was rewarded
with nails dug deep
into my naked forearm.
Thank God, I only said,
"ouch, ouch," while I saw stars
and tried to pull her off
with the other hand
but it took another person
to dig her out of me.
She thought she was being shot
and was grabbing the arm with the gun.
She has been shot many nights
in her wheelchair.
She was fighting for her life
and she won,
sort of.
I was the only one bleeding.

June 3

Mrs. Rodriguez, with an angelic smile,

an Alzheimer's wanderer
who winds up in anybody's bed or bedroom,
happened to wander into the room
of Mrs. Garcia (the pincher).
As the sweet and confused
was being pinched by
the mean and confused,
Mrs. Fulladosa, Garcia's roommate,
began singing Jingle Bells
to add the Fellini touch.

Pulling Rodriguez away,
she began rubbing her injury
as Mrs. Carnero passed by
asking us if we'd seen the baby
she keeps in her room.

"No, Mrs. Carnero, are you sure
you have a baby?"

By this time Mrs. Rodriguez
had wandered toward Jay
who sat guarding his doorway
and pushed her away saying,
"Go on, get out of here."

I put an arm around her waist
and lead her briefly away
from the pain of bitchy woman
and rejecting men.

For a moment
we were two mad sisters,
one due to brain deterioration,
one to impending divorce.

June 7

Today was death watch

for Mrs. Lampert,
an advanced Alzheimer's resident.
Her pulse was so low it did not register.
Her mouth hung open, eyes fixed,
face white from no circulation.
Yet she hung on for hours
as her family gathered around her
and stroked her hair.
When finally the moment came
that she could let go,
everyone sighed.
The family stepped outside
and I and another CNA
performed postmortem care.
We cleaned and dressed her,
tied a towel around her head
to keep her mouth from setting
in the open mouth death pose.
It was like caring for her when she was alive
with something profoundly missing.
Peace lay where Mrs. Lampert used to be
and sadness filled the room.

Later in the hall, Mrs. Rodriguez
mumbled Spanish is a low monotone.
When I leaned my ear close to her mouth
to try and catch a word or two
she kissed me,
as if I had leaned in for that
or if she knew
it was what I needed.

June 9

Mrs. Rixford was caught writing in blood

on her bathroom mirror
with a wound from a razor
stolen from the shower.
We can't read what she was trying to say
but she wears four sets of clothes at once
and she has refused to eat for days.

Mr. Fierro has ripped his catheter
from his urinary tract
and now his penis bleeds.

They are abandoned by their families.
Loneliness is their disease.

Mrs. Rixford is too far away to reach.
Mr. Fierro we are holding
on the brink of a pit.
He responds to attention
and he still eats.

June 10

I have always suspected

that CNAs
recorded meal intakes
without even looking at the plates.
Residents who barely eat anything
at dinner are charted
as eating 100 percent
at breakfast and lunch.
When I ask about this they say,
"Oh they eat better in the morning."
Hmm, okay, maybe
but tonight I noticed on the intake sheet
that Mrs. Lampert, who died three days ago
ate all of her food today.

June 12

Mrs. Hijar would not allow

her restraint to be put back on
after using the bathroom.
"God does not want me to be tied up,"
she said, riled up for a fight.
I went to get help.
Nurse Sharon told her,
"God told me He doesn't want you to fall."
Against her will we tied her in her chair.
When a more humane nurse came on duty
she suggests a "lap buddy,"
a cushion device which fits in front.
Mrs. Hijar was happy.
"Take my hand," she said.
"Don't be afraid."
And I took her hand,
though I remembered the times
she had sliced me with her nails.
Suddenly I said,
"Yo hablo poco español pero
yo estoy aprendiendo mas."
"So you are learning Spanish," she said beaming.
"Yes."
"So you can talk with us?" She radiated
like an angel.
"Si, Manuela, si."

June 17

I saw Mrs. Rodriguez

our innocent, Teresa,
sitting on a love-seat
with Mr. Gallegos
of molesting-aides-in-the-shower-fame.
A large aquarium was between us
but I could lean forward
without being seen.
I felt very protective of Teresa.
Mr. Gallegos patted her thighs,
touched her arm
then held her hands.
Then he waved his hand in front of her face
to test her response.
Next he fondled his crotch.
If he was going to fondle her
I was going to interrupt
but he didn't, this time.
The word is out now.
Mr. Gallegos is after Teresa
and he knows she is not likely
to make a sound
even if he lures her to his room
and rapes her.

June 18

Mrs. Rixford has been casting spells

and putting hexes on us for days.
Tonight she was talking loudly
to herself and hallucinating.
The nurse decided to give her a shot.
Since she was known to get violent
four of us went in.
Immediately she started yelling,
"You're with the FBI.
You're gonna kill me.
There's been an invasion.
My people will get you."
She started swinging her fists
and we held her arms and legs
so the nurse could inject her.
I tried to calm her with a steady voice
telling her, "We're giving you medicine.
We are taking care of you."
But it riled her instead.
"We will torture and kill you.
Me and my army will *take care of you!*"

June 19

The new resident, Mrs. Molero

loves women's breasts.
She always touches
and comments on our *bonita chichitas.*
Today she called mine ripe mangos.
Otherwise she is polite
in her rapid, scrambled Spanish
sprinkled with *"San Antonios."*
She means no harm.
She's an elderly, diseased woman
who happens to like *chichitas.*

June 30

Mrs. Orderica

is dying of cancer
and does not get out of bed.
She rings often.
When I go to her
she has either forgotten
what she wanted
or only wants me there.
She holds my hands
and draws me near.
"You're so sweet," she says.

I think of my private life,
the man who left me
for a bevy of younger women
and I tell her,
"It's so nice to be appreciated.
Thank you."

I think of Mrs. Penwright
who likes to hold my hand
and laugh with me about silly things
and who is afraid of the dark.
And Rose, who is also afraid
and reaches for me.
Minutes at a time
I am famous
in their hearts and minds.

July 1

I found out our new resident,

Mrs. Gragg, is a poet
and story writer
and has all of her wits.
I went to talk to her.
She said she was published
and had archives.
I couldn't wait to see her work.
With a lot of pain
she made her way
over to her computer
and pulled up a file.
It was a story about Jesus
and His greatness.
I had not expected porno
but I was surprised by Jesus.
She went on to tell me
she was an ordained minister
and she blessed me.

I really liked her
but decided not to show her
any of my stories or poems.

July 7

I want a roll call

of the absent
who were briefly here.
I want a black stone wall
etched with their names.
At least let me write them here
so you can read them
or hear me or another read them.
Here are the souls,
roughly 100 years each,
who slipped away in my care
without fanfare or family.

Mrs. Acosta, who tweaked my nose
and taught me my first Spanish words.
Mrs. Lankford, who stopped in the middle
of a word salad to call my name.
Mrs. Esquival, who called me an angel
until the pain got too bad.
Mrs. Regalardo, who sang "Sweet Mary" to me
and clung to me like a child.
Mrs. Martin, who called 911 and asked,
"Did you know I was here all alone?"
then handed the phone to me.

Something resonated in my bones
all the way through the cosmos.

The death of a twenty year old marriage
is indeed a death.
Trying to find words to tell you
I awake to a loneliness
even a full day with purpose
does not shake
and to a grief
even this transient
but transcendental love
cannot quell.

I am alone here.

July 14

Teresa is in a vest restraint now,

tied to a chair
because chemical restraints
make her fall down.

She lives a life of vague fear
and total confusion,
prisoner to the likes of me
who would free her
if I were not restrained myself.

While removing her bra,
getting her ready for bed,
she became agitated.
I suspect she had been molested,
got hysterical
and was drugged
but this is only a suspicion.

At this point in her life
the best thing she could do
is remember the happy past
if there was any
and if she could.

August 9

Today was my last day.

It would be cruel
to tell them I am leaving.
They have lost so much already.

I have worked as a CNA
to test my sincerity
and toughen me
for a medical profession.
I have gone from tenderfoot,
nauseous at the smells and sights
to the steel-willed empathy
it takes to perform well
and with kindness.
Blood, vomit, urine, feces,
attacks, cursing,
are simple facts of the situation.

Beds empty and are refilled.
The cycle of life goes on.
We hold their hands and love them
in a special way
but we do not mourn deeply
on their passing.
We did not know them
in their lives,
only in their dying.
They go to a better place
whether it is "heaven"
or simply
an end to suffering.

We all go on
somehow.

Drawing by El Paso artist **Lemuel Arredondo**. Arredondo has worked as an artist for *Fusion* magazine and his work has been exhibited at several venues including El Paso Artist Association and the University of Texas at El Paso.

Bibliography

The Nurnberg Poems, No Press, 1983

Lady in Red and White, Northern Pressure Press, 1984

Fighting Woman, Planet Detroit Chapbooks, 1986

Eye of the Beast (w/ Robert Burlingame, S. Ramnath, and Lyn Lifshin), Vergin' Press, 1986

Virgin Mary and Madonna (w/Lyn Lifshin), Vergin' Press, 1986

He Dreams His Playmate, Ghost Dance #42, 1987

Body Parts, Krax Publications (England), 1987

Skin Divers (w/Lyn Lifshin), Krax Publications, 1988

The Jesuit Poems (w/Lyn Lifshin), Implosion Press, 1989

The Innocents (w/Lyn Lifshin), Buzzard's Roost Press, 1991

Home is Where You Are: Conversations with the Homeless, Buzzard's Roost Press, 1991

Halloween: Notes on Demons, Buzzard's Roost Press, 1991

The Purple Keeper, Art: Mag, 1992

Too Hot for Speech, Krax Publications, 1992

Dik-Dik, Hyacinth House Publications, 1993

Naughty Broads (w/ Ana Christy, Sara Consla, and Alexia Lyn Dolton), Implosion Press, 1994

Finding Reality in Myth: Travels with Belinda, Chiron Review Press, Winner of 1995 *Chiron Review* Chapbook Contest

Notes of a Human Warehouse Engineer, Liquid Paper Press, Winner of 1998 *Nerve Cowboy* Chapbook Contest

Late Night in the Psych Ward, Lummox Press, 2001

Wet Moments (designed by Didi Menendez, photos by Cheryl Townsend), Lulu.com, 2008

Blue Rooms, Black Holes, White Lights, Unlikely Books, 2009, 2016

Kaleidoscope Dharma, Red Mare #12, 2017

Other Titles from Unlikely Books

We'll See Who Seduces Whom by Tom Bradley

_a ship on the line by Vincent A. Cellucci and Christopher Shipman

Scorpions by Joel Chace

Love and Other Lethal Things by K. R. Copeland

ANCHOR WHAT by Vernon Frazer

Definitions of Obscurity by Vernon Frazer and Michelle Greenblatt (Second Edition of *Dark Hope,* Argotist E-Books)

ASHES AND SEEDS by Michelle Greenblatt

brain : storm by Michelle Greenblatt (Second Edition, originally anabasis Press)

pleth by j/j hastain and Marthe Reed

anonymous gun. by Kurtice Kucheman (Second Edition)

Monolith by Anne McMillen (Second Edition)

When Red Blood Cells Leak by Anne McMillen (Second Edition)

Ghazals 1-59 and Other Poems by Sheila E. Murphy and Michelle Greenblatt

#specialcharacters by Larissa Shmailo

Apocalyptics by C. Derick Varn

Beautiful Rush by Marc Vincenz

Gods of a Ransacked Century by Marc Vincenz

Pachuco Skull with Sombrero: Los Angeles, 1970 by Lawrence Welsh

Made in the USA
Columbia, SC
11 February 2023